# HAPPINESS, SADNESS, AND ALL THINGS IN BETWEEN

**The University of Lincoln** is a bright and modern university at the heart of a historic city, rising fast in the ranks to the top 30 for student satisfaction in the UK, and top 20 for Creative Writing. Our team of award-winning professional writers pride themselves on preparing our students for life beyond university, readying them for a career in writing or publishing at the same time as honing their craft. It's an exciting place to be.

**UNIVERSITY OF LINCOLN**

LINCOLN SCHOOL OF
CREATIVE ARTS

ISBN: 978-1-916938-99-1

Cover designed by Aaron Kent

Typeset by Aaron Kent

Broken Sleep Books Ltd
Rhydwen
Talgarreg
Ceredigion
SA44 4HB

Broken Sleep Books Ltd
Fair View
St Georges Road
Cornwall
PL26 7YH

# Happiness, Sadness, and All Things In Between

---

Edited by
*Fee Griffin*

Broken Sleep University Press

# Contents

## Foreword

It's a corny thing to say, but this bunch of students is very special to me. You know what? I'm going to give myself a 'corny' pass for the exact length of this foreword, so strap in. The fact is, these writers are an incredibly talented and versatile group. So versatile, in fact, that I'm frustrated you're only getting one dose of each! You love X's short story? You should try their poetry! You think Y's non-fiction is good? Get a load of this script... the good news is, I have confidence we won't have to wait long until these authors publish again. Excitingly, I know of a handful of submissions already in progress, both individual pieces and full-length works. Some of these authors have already been published in journals, placed in competitions, etc. Others rounded off their last week of lectures by interviewing for publishing jobs, planning out their route into copywriting, or launching submissions for their own anthologies—this time as editor. Still more are continuing on to MAs and we're lucky enough to be looking forward to another year with many of them here at Lincoln.

But back to this book. Much as I want to, I can't list everyone by name here and take you though what's great about their work; that discovery is yours to enjoy. But I do want to give you an idea of the range of ideas you'll encounter here: two astronauts eating cha siu bao in the forest; a head in a bottle bank; a swimming pool full of indigestion tablets; a poisoner in the court of Elizabeth I; a laundry basket full of bones; a waltz with a cash register; a menopause in poetry; girlbreath on glass; fat ghosts... can you feel the quality?

When I began lecturing in creative writing, in 2020, I was a total beginner, and *these* were the kinds of ideas I had the pleasure of reading. I used to bore people about how good they were, in much the same way that people will bore you about a favourite cat, film director, or weather pattern. Watching as these writers have honed their craft and inspired and influenced each other (and me) has been the most enormous pleasure for me over the last three years. I'm excited that Aaron Kent, the editor of Broken Sleep Books, has read their work and decided to publish it. I'm excited that you are reading it, now. But most of all, and like all good books, this one makes me excited for what the authors will write next...

— Fee Griffin

# Five Poems

## Olivia Ansdell

## It'll never last

*It'll never last*, they smirk
Spectators to a day they weren't invited to

A closed-off bar for sober mums
Scrambled for the last drop at breakfast

Lovesick and dizzy she floats down the aisle
*You'd have thought she would've lost weight for the wedding*
I'm a cartoon rabbit and you're the meat pie on the windowsill to cool

The first dance
A room of hungry onlookers
Their jealous mumbling
Rumbling louder than the music

It'll never last, they spit
But we can't hear from laughing

## *Extra pickles and a large Fanta*
## *for mixer please*

You visit me in my sleep and are always there waiting for me
Every time I look in the mirror and every time I drink a glass of wine on
my own

There's no funeral so I'm left to celebrate your life in my bedroom
Alone I hold your wake in my pyjamas
I toast you with the dirty plates and the crumbs in my bed

You speak every time I'm sorry for making a scene in Mcdonalds
Swaying whilst ordering a McPlant
I apologise and I'm eleven again
Watching your mum telling mine not to drink so fast

## *The divorce and I live alone*

Together we're wrapped in overcast
I can hear the lifeboats in the distance
But the lifeboats are too far away
It wears your shoes and they're too small
But the divorce is a real Cinderella

The bed is empty and I can't sleep

## *Untitled*

Does it hurt? I asked
Huh?
Oh that!

We both look at it, crunching at the bones in her hand, blood dripping
from its mouth
I nodded

Not really, although I've never really thought about it, she replied
It doesn't do it all the time, please don't worry
I promise I'm fine; can I get you a drink?

But it's taken your whole arm!
Yes, but I have another, she said, holding up her hand of wriggling    fingers

## Untitled Haiku

A reflection on my future
Her glancing but sour charm
As she bites into another sucker

# Five Poems

Rebecca Holding

## *on daydreaming*

when i was a kid // i dreamed of being // a bird // on whose wings // spanned the horizon // whose directional // abilities // were not restricted // by the x and y // axes // now that i am older // i dream of being // a cat // one who can sleep // all day // without judgement // one who does not know // about pandemics // and war and crime and // crying // until you cannot // breathe, until you can- // -not sleep, until you // cannot see until // all you can do // is wish // to be // a cat

## *on bridges and overhangs*

get in line, dear // for me // the hatred // the need // the desperation // i can hear it all // to begin with // it must be a stroke of fate that someone was out here // that i saw her at all // that she fell in the outskirts of town // that my arms aren't long enough to reach // but it's not my fault // to be watching her drown like this // oh // and she's calling for me // that she's awake to call for help is a miracle // the fall must've hurt // the coughs and noises of pain // the gasps for air // for me? // she reaches outward and upwards // the water camouflaging her // staining her // from here it looks like oil

*on my 18th birthday*

when new

ar     e

imagined

Dawn leaves her

hopeless                    she runs

and follows      to                              assist

accident                s

to find the

trouble              d

to    rescue                          the angered

to escape

the    Dawn                                    and

her       pa  i  n.

sh        e                                    is

not ready    t  o

fly

Source: https://www.pokemon.com/uk/
pokemon-episodes/10_01-following-a-maidens-voyage/

# *on the importance of fictional characters*

the comfort that comes
from someone hitting rock bot-
-tom and surviving

## *on broken glass*

cherish him // him // because he's forgotten to cherish himself // the
broken parts of him that will never fit back together // the way he will
never be whole again // every one of you // in the way only he can // in
the way he has cherished you // you don't know // what he would've done
// to feel // to be thought of that way // cherish him for who is // who will
ever be // who has ever been // every possible version of him that could
exist // the broken boy // the hopeless child // who found the strength to
become who you know now // the fighter // the indomitable spirit that
doesn't know how to lie down and give up // whilst you can // whilst you
have him // forevermore // cherish him before you lose him // please

# Daddy Issues
## (Three Poems)

## Phoebe McBurney

## an advert break for meaningless words

my first experience of grief as a child
was not a transfusion to the earth below
but the realisation that my dad would never be
what he should be  / what i wanted him to be /
what i needed him to be  / and the worst part
was not the desolation of unwantedness
i felt when he left but the bliss that dawned
the second he was gone /

# *until next time*

'y o u ' l l    r e g r e t    i t    o n c e    i ' m    g o n e'
'you'll extinguish the burning house
no longer nauseated by weighted black smoke
curling round the corners of the door frame
while i abused your mum behind floral walls
my son just sat and watched /

you'll see the shadow of your nine-year-old self
and reminisce on the first time i was
brave enough to tell you that you gained weight
that you don't smile properly in photos
and that you bite your cheeks and nails too much /

you'll forget my reminder at thirteen
that i just wanted you to be a pretty girl
by that point you're already pinching
your underdeveloped skin in the mirror
and binning half of your sandwich at school /

you'll be excited to phone up and boast your grades
and i'll boast what a clever granddaughter you are
until you become clever enough to deconstruct
the claws from the air in my lungs
the hydraulic press of false accusations /

you'll diminish my poison with
sixteen years of trauma streaming down
your acned cheeks;
the phoneline crackling under vultures' wings
i'll repeat the same thing over and over –
        'liarliarliarliarliarliar'
your dad never left you avoided you, stole,
abused, manipulated, gaslighted you
class c /class b / class a

28

he loves you
i love you
c h i l d /

you'll only spend years and years
andyearsandyearsandyearsandyears
questioning if it ever was your fault
choking yourself with your lack of guilt
as soon as you hear i'm gone' /

*grandfather -*
*where were smartphones when i really needed them? –*
*an incendiary to leave recording on a leather sofa arm;*
*i knew the hurricanes he'd hurl*
*i started bottling them in labelled vials as i got older*
*and finally*
*what i thought would've congealed to blood*
*spewed out as saltwater /*

## *live laugh loathe*

i need you all to kindly
s h u t
    t h e
   f u c k    u p
for a goddamn second
and stop chasing me around
this glass-stained untruth
stop making me pressure-wash
my face until its smooth enough
to crease in all the right places
stop making me have to come up with
three meals
    a    d  a  y
and piss at inconvenient times /

stop making my feet trail on the concrete
in small dissociative footsteps
working like the fairytales told me to
waltzing with dusty floors and cash registers
and the hormones of evil step-karens
handling more money in an hour than i'll
make in a month but it's okay because
i'm not doing it in a false-consciousness
kind of way but in an undiscovered celebrity
kind of way – one who goes home and drinks
heavy metal to the sound of a wine glass
and melts their eyeliner off before they
even get into the shower /

stop making me disable my humanity
and break my soul beneath shrivelling kneecaps

scooping my ankles out with a metal spoon
to be used / misused / used / misused

be deprived of money for rent
whilst an old bald white man somewhere
rubs his silk-sheet hands with sanitised dollars
fucking with who and what he wants and
writing puppet shows for his island-hopping friends
who want to unravel my dna and recoil
back fifty years where you could pin my
protruding stomach to death with a smile
deluding that you shook god's hand /

stop making me pretend that the world isn't
on fire and people aren't dying and they're
not hungry or homeless or scared or that
gay people aren't prisoners and people of
colour aren't villains and the rich don't
kill the poor and women aren't sacrificed and that
those with the crowns can't ever read the scriptures wrong /

s  t  o  p /

# The Lady with the Lamp

## Rhys Pattison

# The Lady with the Lamp

This creative text is a non-fiction diary that reflects the character of Florence Nightingale, showing both her strength and flaws. This includes an expression of her racism in words such as 'Savages'.

*October 15th, 1854*
*Wednesday,*
*18:56*

The people of this fine nation, the Englishmen have been in an uproar since the battle of Alma, where their sick and injured soldiers had been left to rot in a filthy establishment. An establishment that has been neglected due to poor planning from this government. Shameful. To save face, Sidney Herbert, secretary of war sent me a letter; she requested that I, Florence Nightingale assemble a group of the best nurses to travel with me to the battlefield of Crimea. It may take quite some time to find adequate nurses.

*October 16th, 1854*
*Thursday*
*17:40*

I managed to pull some strings and have organised a group of 34 brave nurses from varied religious backgrounds, to make the trip to the British base hospital stationed in Constantinople. Within a few short days, these nurses and I will begin our journey but first, we must prepare both our equipment and our mind, for I suspect that this make-shift hospital will have some of the most unsanitary conditions I will have ever seen. I believe this is my calling, a sign from the Holy Father himself.

*October 21st – 23rd, 1854*
*Monday - Wednesday,*
*18: 41*

We set sail. The other nurses and I will arrive in Malta first, where we will replenish our supplies and hopefully find a ship that isn't infested with cockroaches. The second day of our voyage begins with a brutal storm, the sea is shaking the ship with such violence that I fear it may tear it apart. While the storm outside continues another brews within me. I cannot take much more of this; I hope for all our sakes that we make it to land soon. We arrive in Malta; it would have been nice to place my weary feet on some dry land. However, I was bedbound.

*November 3rd, 1854*
*Friday,*
*17:30*

It's been a couple of hours since we left the port, I hope we get there soon. We are halfway through our journey, and I have spent most of that time locked in my berthing. I understand that travel by sea is the quickest, but my innards cannot take much more of this. Finally, we arrived at the Crimean port and already I can see the effects of this war, plastered onto the faces of our soldiers. With my stomach on the road to recovery, the nurses and I wait. It would seem that we all have the same thought ravaging our minds.

*Now the real battle begins.*

*November 4th, 1854*
*Saturday,*
*18: 51*

Upon arrival at the hospital, the other nurses and I discovered that the conditions were much worse than we were led to believe, we were stunned. The hospital itself resembled more of a prison, you wouldn't even send a barbarian here, let alone a soldier of the great British Empire. To make matters worse there was a downpour, we were soaked to the bone and the sludge that it had created filled the cesspit where this makeshift hospital sat; the smell was rancid, and the central yard had become a sea of refuse. Though the rats seemed to be enjoying themselves.

As we made our way further into the hospital, it revealed more of its hideous colours. One of the orderlies, an elderly attendant, briefly greeted us before rushing back to their assigned ward. They are supposed to be the ones keeping this hospital sanitary. But by the looks of them they had never touched soap in their lives, what should I expect from one of the barbaric natives of this accursed land. When some time had passed, we were finally shown our temporary lodging. Our journey was long and arduous, so we were expecting some much-deserved food. To our surprise they didn't even have cooking utensils. Our first day here has been disappointing, it looks like I'll have to step up and make some changes around here.

*November 5th, 1854*
*Sunday,*
*18:55*

On day two we received our less than warm welcome. I decided to have a look around the different wards of this hospital. After the second ward, it became blatantly obvious that there were no beds or furniture of any kind; soldiers had been eating, sleeping, and even defecating in the same place. I was appalled, this was indeed no way for a functioning hospital to behave. Once I had flagged down one of those uncivilised orderlies, I learned that this hospital was once a barracks which explains why there have been so many fatalities and the absolute disregard for hygiene.

With this new information in mind, I continued my inspection of each ward. That was until I came across an out-of-place hatch, tucked away deep within the back of this hospital. Since I was not familiar with how barracks are supposed to be set out, I did what was natural and opened it, but that soon proved to be a mistake. I was not ready for the horrors that were hiding down there. Two hundred of those vulgar natives, many of which I presume were being used as prostitutes. They were sat in their own filth, some of them dying. I dared not venture any further out of fear that the miasma would take me as well. For now, I have quarantined them.

November 6<sup>th</sup>, 1854
*Monday,*
18:57

It was our third day, and only now was I meeting the other doctors and those in charge. First was the Commissariat, this elderly man, who bought the rations, and the equipment had a very pompous attitude. After him, I met Dr Andrew Smith the acting Director General, alongside a few of the surgeons. I had gathered them by our accommodation, and they refused to acknowledge us. They didn't really approve of us being here nor do they believe that we will be of any use. I will show them how wrong they are.

Although our conversation was brief, I came to a quick understanding of just how this hospital had failed to aid these injured soldiers. Because of the ever-increasing number of sick soldiers. Plus, the doctor's refusal for nurses meant that the workload had simply become too much. So much so that they had started to delegate important tasks to the unqualified, uneducated barbarians that they had running around. Thanks to my investigations I have discovered that the rations for food and equipment are in constant short supply. I must order some more, but judging by the thousands of soldiers we have in our care, we will need a surplus. However, the army funds will not be enough to cover the cost, we have no other choice but to dive into the civilian fund. It looks like we will have our work cut out for us.

*November 10ᵗʰ, 1854*
*Friday,*
*19:05*

When I first arrived here, I saw just how poorly this hospital was run, I saw how we were in constant short supply of even the most basic of things. It was appalling, so I took it upon myself to order more or at least I tried, but I was stopped. Prevented by the Army Officials, the very people who were supposed to take care of their men. They refused to use civilian funds to buy the equipment we need, now I fear that what I brought with me as well as what we already have will not be enough.

*November 17ᵗʰ, 1854*
*Friday,*
*19:35*

A week has passed since we arrived at the barrack hospital and not a single doctor, surgeon or even kitchen staff have made use of us. I understand that we are not welcome here, but we're talking about the lives of soldiers, how could they put those poor men's lives on the line for something as simple as their hurt pride? For now, I have sent the nurses I brought with me to stand at the hospital and wait for when a doctor calls upon them. I fear that is all I can do at this moment.

*December 17ᵗʰ, 1854*
*Sunday,*
*19:34*

We have been here a month. This is getting ridiculous, every day I send my nurses out to await instruction or to offer their help to the doctors, yet they refuse to make use of us. The useless orderlies, whose job it is to keep this hospital clean and keep its patients clean are clearly not doing their job. So, I have taken it upon myself to show those barbarians how to do their job. I have ordered the remaining nurses to sort through the linen to make slings, anything to keep us busy, anything to keep these soldiers alive. I have procured the necessary equipment and food regardless of how the officials feel.

Many of the brave women I brought with me are starting to feel as though they have accomplished nothing. Many have wondered if there was even a point in leaving England in the first place and in all honesty, I cannot blame them for that. The management around here is corrupt.

Something needs to change. If I am the one that will have to change it, then I will do what I must with the limited power that I hold, even if I have to work through the night.

It has been a few days since writing in this diary, but I have been busy. In my last update, I wrote about how the central figures around here are against us. They have made it their mission to see us fail. But I have a mission of my own and I have executed it perfectly. First and foremost, the cleanliness of the hospital was atrocious. I could not bear to look at it anymore. So, I requested a hundred scrubs and brushes then ordered some of the nurses alongside some of the soldiers (those who were capable) to help me scrub this dump clean. By the time we had finished, no one would believe this was the same hospital we walked into.

After ensuring that the hospital was spick and span, I moved my attention to the dietary requirements of certain soldiers; many of these soldiers had either been fed food they cannot eat or not fed at all. Any decent medical professional would know that wounds do not heal on an empty stomach however, I ran into yet another issue or rather many issues. As it turns out, the kitchen staff do not have all the utensils, when I inquired about this, I was of course turned away. Though the utensils would be nice they are not a necessity. After all, we will stir a pot with a stick if we have to. But the one problem that will continue to be a pain in my side, is the written order that I will need from the patients' doctors. Every time I look for them, they are nowhere to be found. I understand that they may be busy, but aftercare is just as important as pre-operation, and it is our job as nurses to provide such care.

December 21<sup>st</sup>, 1854
Thursday,
20:29

The war seems to be getting worse and the number of wounded pouring in keeps increasing. I can see on the doctor's faces, that they are struggling to keep up with this many while also refusing our help. If another flood of patients arrives, then I'm not sure that they will hold out. I have told the nurses to continue waiting, and I'm sure any day now they will be begging for our assistance. Anyway, lately I have been patrolling each of the wards within the hospital, checking every night on every patient new and old; it's about that time again.

*December 22<sup>nd</sup>, 1854*

*Friday,*

*20:30*

The doctors cannot take it anymore, so they gave in. Now, we can use our full potential as nurses and this foolish standoff can come to an end. The nurses feel like they are finally being of some use. I don't know how long this war will last, or how long we will be told to stay here but what I do know, is that we are going to get very busy. It's about time I start to make my rounds, after all I am as the patients call me...

'The lady with the lamp'.

# Hampton Court Palace

## Catherine Arkley

# Hampton Court Palace

I saw more than any others ever did in court; past the corsets, lace garters and lead-finished porcelain skin. It was my honor since birth to serve the Queen. My mother had done so before and I was chosen next. Elizabeth always claimed it was my eccentric nature that drew her in; some called me erratic, but they knew better than to say it to my face. I'd grown up in court, learning from my mother, and started serving the Queen, taking her position, at sixteen.

The Queen took after her father in some ways: his fiery ambition to be best above all others, his impetuous commissions of death. A Spanish envoy had been beheaded, days after his arrival in the past week; all it had taken was a small gesture to the guards. Being so elegant about death nurtured fear in others. To me, it lit a flame of passion. An ember burning bright in admiration.

Things changed when he visited at the start of the month. The great renowned adventurer, Walter Raleigh. Not worthy of the Queen's eye and attention. Reckless and unfaithful. His wandering eyes stabbing through my back into the Queen's heart. Wounding her soul irreparably in every move. Twisting the dagger in his frivolity. Then laying his coat over a puddle, as if to exempt all his pain caused with ignorance.

I would have to eliminate him soon. He took my place. My intimacy on the Queen's side. The consequences were as clear as the crystals embedded in her jewelry. The emeralds were as deep as my jealousy and rubies as fiery as the passion and flames filling my soul. All so fragile and precious, just as the body they lay on.

This morning, I saw the switch, the way she fretted over her hair being placed to perfection, instructing each pearl-ended pin to be delicate and notable to the eye. The reality that Raleigh was after her wealth and power was apparent to her. But still, she yearned for his attention. The way I yearned for hers.

The other maids caught hold of my perturbance that day, as my face betrayed my seething discontent and my knuckles whitened into tight fists. I snatched the tray, crystal goblets and a carafe of wine, it rattled a little. I steadied myself, I couldn't allow my anger to break the goblets or spill the wine. As I strode out towards the grand dining hall the echoes of laughter consumed my mind whole.

She sat at the end of the table. A great throne chair, with floral patterns etched into the mahogany frame, and a quilted velvet cushion throughout. I paced a little, fearing her impatience. I couldn't fall out of favor. Placing the tray in front of her, our eyes met. Her eyes appeared like molten pools of amber. The coldness they held stung a little, but I knew, she should not be seen to show affection to me. I told myself, several times daily. She cannot, but she cares. She does. She does. She does.

She must.

The anger would engulf me, on those occasions when I couldn't compete with my mind and reassure myself: the Queen's true reason for never marrying and bearing an heir, was not a lack of suitors, was not her interest in Raleigh, but was her love for me. I was her true love that she could not conform to, because the world could never understand our connection. I was the secret tale that would remain unseen in the history books of the future. A figure in a picture, of whom they'd never know the real importance.

I would see to it that Raleigh was sent away, the courtiers would no doubt want the same; Elizabeth philandering with a reckless explorer reflected her as weak. A position she could not be in at a time of such threat, such danger to her authority. The courtiers had already been pushing for war against the Spanish, but the English were outnumbered in resources. The Queen needed my help now more than ever. I wouldn't fail her.

First, I would have to plant the idea in court. I'd spread rumours of Raleigh, not that he required much help with acquiring attention. But none the less, if the court doubted him more and more, they would see fit to have him removed. The Queen would never suspect me, her most loyal follower, of hurting her. I didn't want to hurt her, of course, but I needed to, for her own protection. Perhaps if she heard more of his dalliances, she would see him for the criminal he is, and call for some action to be taken herself.

Yes, the Queen beheading Raleigh himself. Beautiful. Blissful. Sweet joy. The perfection of that idea was simply too exquisite not to bring a smile to spread across my lips. She caught sight, coughing to catch my attention, then nodding her head at the wine to signal me to pour.

"What has you smiling Avery?"

I picked up the carafe of wine carefully, filling her goblet to just below the brim, wiping the spout with a cloth to stop the dripping.

"Oh, it is nothing your Majesty."

She pulled back in her chair, scraping against the floor. "Take the tray to the kitchens."

I picked up the tray, holding my gaze on it, I heard her delicate footsteps echoing mine as we walked away in opposite directions. She would most likely be heading to the stables for a ride with her favorite horse Bayard. She rode regularly, as of late. Perhaps it was the strain. I knew well for Elizabeth things felt different when riding. The wind flowing through her hair, focusing on the speed and rhythm, and her mind distracted wholly as a result.

I was to collect dresses from London today on her behalf. It was my job, as she knew my hands could handle the expensive and luxurious materials. The others had tried before, but the dresses had reached the palace with scuffs of mud and small tears. Besides, I enjoyed talking to the dressmaker; she had all the town's gossip, which the Queen would no doubt devour when I returned.

This would be the perfect opportunity to start spreading the rumours of the Queen's dalliance with Raleigh. Once the gossip reached her, the whispers would spread like lightning through the town, then through the whole kingdom, until all that was left would be vast shame.

Upon arrival the dressmaker led me to the dresses of finest satin, silk, and velvet. Her forehead crinkled up as she looked my way, accessing the skirt of my dress perhaps.

"What on earth happened to that dress?" She asked.

I smiled. "We both know my skirts are the least interesting thing to discuss here,"

She raised her eyebrow. "What would you rather discuss?"

"Tell me your knowings of Sir Raleigh,"

"The girls in the whore houses seem rather fond of him, more than a few of his bastards will be running around the summer next,"

I wound my hair around my finger. "I see,"

"Why do you ask?"

I wound my hair tighter letting the tip of my finger begin to go a mottled purple. "It seems the Queen has developed an interest in him as of late."

She gave a curt nod knowing my intention in telling her what I knew.

The dressmaker left to another room bringing the Queen's dresses in boxes. I gave her a curt nod. She hadn't told any news that was new as such. The women wouldn't dare say if Raleigh had bedded them, most were brought by their desperation for money. Raleigh had enough wealth to keep somewhat hidden.

The carriage drew up in the palace gardens. The horses halted in the gravel. As I stepped down from the carriage, I smelled the lavender lingering around me. My pace quickening in excitement to discuss Raleigh with the Queen while she admired her new dresses. I reached the hall. Her soft laughter filled my senses. My feet were pacing away, with no control towards her. She was there, laid on a chaise longue, her back arched and his hand tracing lines over her jaw. My fears were no longer false truths. They were real, it was real. How could she betray me? It couldn't have been her doing, he must have manipulated her actions. I caught her eye for a moment, then turned.

I took the dresses to her room, trying to convince myself what I'd seen was all an illusion, a cruel trick my mind played. Her steps sounded over the stone staircase.

She faced me head-on. "Avery, tomorrow Raleigh will be knighted, prepare it."

I hesitated a moment, my mind distorted, the words came out. "Yes ma'am."

Inside, the screams were louder than any of my words. I turned, walking towards the doorway, bowing as I left for the kitchens. Then I saw him. Across the hall, his eyes following my every move, telling me all I required to know. The whole time, that savage had witnessed it all. His smugness still visible.

The small knife I'd attached to my wrist with a leather-bound case tickled me. It was a contraption I'd found in the market. An Italian seller claiming the design itself was Da Vinci's best. A sharp blade, short but longer than a dagger. Able to shroud itself under a sleeve and be pulled out in a moment of need. I'd told the seller it was for my husband, a man that, truthfully no longer existed. Men always thought women were simple, and it would always end in their downfall, as far as I was concerned.

My steps fell heavy against the stone, a warning perhaps to the staff who were coming, or perhaps my body's attempt to release some of the anger that pulsed through it. I reached the kitchens, the staff stood in neat lines. They knew if I appeared here this late it wouldn't be a simple matter. They would be burdened with preparing enough dishes and decoration for a ceremony in a matter of hours. It roused excitement in me, knowing I could simply snap my fingers and they would scatter like mice.

I had always longed for power. Control. Force.

I made orders for which goblets should be used, and which meals to be prepared. Then left the room. My God, being surrounded by such struggle was exhausting. I went to my chambers, laying my head down, letting my weary eyes close for a few moments. The morning came soon after. The day had come, there was no time. Final strikes, must always be quick.

Attacking Raleigh would be too obvious, I'd be caught and defenseless. Perhaps I could delay things at the very least. A small tincture in his wine. Just enough to cause sickness to not create suspicion. Then I'd have time to convince the advisors to the Queen to send Raleigh to explore on her behalf or onto a ship against the Spaniards.

The Ipomoea plant I'd collected from the woods would work. A plant which would result in hallucinations and severe physical illness. Enough to delay Raleigh. Although, I'd need one of the other maids to take it, he'd question my serving him. I was the Queen's servant, and as such only served her needs. I felt perhaps he'd started to sense my disregard towards him, my emotions were hard to keep hidden. My face, my mannerisms, my speech, it all echoed and beckoned the seething hate I'd built up inside to the surface.

He'd spoken of The Indies before to the Queen, filling her mind with fanciful ideas of owning a land she had no knowledge of. He was the only one who had been there, his crew were loyal and, every claim he made, they'd back. Lies or truths. But would the Queen ever question his words? Would she see the ambition that lingered all over his acts like a sort of miasma? The man only cared for himself, that much was clear to me. To the Queen, I suppose she saw his acts as for our great nation. But Britain wouldn't be as favorable next to Raleigh on paper in the end.

I couldn't help but let a grin take over, as I faced the mirror, imagining him in agony and embarrassment. On the floor, crying out for help. Finally, getting some punishment. Letting the Queen be open to interception once more. Now I would have her full attention. The time to show her how repulsive and pathetic he was. The time to let him go.

The tincture of Ipomea was being served up now. He just had to take it.

A shriek bounced through the palace halls, reaching my room, bending through the corridors, a beautiful cacophony of terror. I paced up the steps towards Raleigh's room in feigned horror as to not give a suggestion of my true intentions. The maid kneeling beside him turned her head, forcing our eyes to meet.

I stooped beside her, sensing her eyes would see through my lies and into my soul's desires if her glare lasted any longer. I pulled her back, wrenching her arms off his chest. Probably another poor soul Raleigh had enticed in a few moments' manipulation disguised as intimacy.

"Let go for goodness sake."

"No—"

"She'll be here soon."

She moved away then knowing the rath of the Queen would be far worse than mine, being witnessed fawning all over a royal guest, further so when that guest was held in high favor. That was considered no simple mistake when being punished. The maid and I knew this too well, the best outcome would be expulsion from the palace with no doors open to employment following. Perhaps swift death was more merciful than leaving culprits to struggle a longer more painful path to death.

I turned back, facing Raleigh on the floor, his eyes attempting to flitter open with no luck and groans of pain as he clung to his stomach calling out for help. I wondered if he could sense my presence, my smugness creeping its way over my skin, the hairs on my arms standing up in exhilaration. I pointed towards the bed indicating to the maid to move him before I left.

I traced my fingertips across the banister, I'd achieved what I'd wanted, but now I had to cover what I'd done. Nobody could trace it back. I'd call on the palace physician first, Gregor, an old man who'd lived in the palace beyond my time. I sensed he'd be senile enough to not to think much of what had happened but rather give Raleigh a few tinctures to cure what afflictions he could see.

Reaching his chambers, I knocked three times rapidly; he would have to sense some urgency to move at any great pace. His heavy plods reached the door, a lock turned, and the frame creaked as he faced me. Rubbing his head and placing his costruktio on for better vision, he began his usual drivel.

"Avery, it's rather early is it not?"

"Yes, it is, there's been an incident—"

"With whom?"

"With Raleigh."

# 6 Poems on the Menopause

## Amanda Austen

# David & Goliath

At the entrance, like David and Goliath
in a tennis match
students she could have given birth to pass by

        itdoesntmatteritmattersitdoesntmatteritmatters

Did she remember to stick on her patch?
the one the doctor eventually prescribed
his compassion missing from his certificate on the wall
a man would never survive / she didn't think / she would survive

        youwontIwillyouwontIwillyouwontIwillyouwont

she might as well go in
she could sit at the back of the lecture
she could always make an excuse and leave
he asked her why she decided to study a degree

        shesaidshewasrefusingtobedefinedbytheperimenopause

she waited for laughter / she got encouragement / flushed red / cried /
forgot her
words / fought fatigue / but at last /

        she     was     alive     again

*Costa*

she sits          by the fountain          at costa          a soft breeze
blowing tendrils of     red hair      sunglasses hide      her dull     tired eyes
all around her     is children's laughter          friends' chatter     buzzing mobiles
she listens

                    invisible

disconnected                                              anesthetized

                              alone

nudge the sun     aside          her watch               stops     ticking
she walks     amongst strangers          and continues     searching     for
herself     amongst          the          shelves     in          the     chemist

                                                  the clouds

# I bought a puppy

| | | | |
|---|---|---|---|
| I never longed    for you until it / | was | too | late |
| I thought when I didn't have a choice / it | would | be | easier |
| I watched others hold their / | bundle | of | treasure |
| tiny rosebud lips suckling their / | white | milky | breast |
| I heard voices / question / and | bought | a | puppy |
| I failed expectations / and | ignored | raised | eyebrows |
| I was childless / | young | and | fertile |
| until my body / | became | an | enemy |
| hormones in the ring in / | the | red | corner |
| The *change* / said the | boards | they | paraded |
| In scantily / clad outfits | with | no | gloves |
| Too late / the crowds | jeered | and | shouted |
| referee holding / Menopause arm | in | the | air |
| I long for you / amongst the barren | field | of | dreams |
| as I walk / my | dog | in | season |

53

## I tried

I tried to tell her about the change          she laughed and continued texting her mates
I tried to explain about the anxiety          she laughed and continued drinking shots
I tried to tell her about the symptoms          she laughed and celebrated her 21st birthday
I tried to tell her time goes too quickly          she laughed and told me life starts at 40
I tried to tell her why she felt so bad          she cried and stared right through me

I

tried

# Untitled

| | |
|---|---|
| It looks like me/ the girl in the mirror | paleskinredstraightcurlsdulleyes |
| lips cracked/ framing words | inabrokensentence |
| grasping at/ slippery eels | forthestolenones |
| I'm missing/ something crucial | anincompletesetofwiresapatchshortonaquilt |
| I am there/but missing | presentbutnotcorrect |
| I Google how/ to find | someonewhoislost |
| I write down/ a number | forthepolicestation |
| I call them/ to report | amissingperson |
| They/ask/ who is missing | Igivemyname |
| A doctor/ with a leaflet | spurtsprojectilevomit |
| I leave the room / suggesting | herdiplomaneedsrinsinginbleach |

# Numbers

16 rain drops, race down the windowpane

12 leaves, snatched from the oak tree

2 dogs, sniff the hedgerow

6 clouds, embrace the sun

5 cars, pass her house

8 ants, scurry along the patio

3 birds, peck at the fat balls

1 cat, watches them

12 pegs, hold no clothing

10 messages, flash on her phone

4 letters, lay on the doormat

15 symptoms, battled this month

30 tablets, lined up on the table like soldiers

# The Moon and Her Man

## Charlotte Brown

# The Moon and her Man

Andy isn't going to Lucien's birthday party tonight. A few months ago, his best friend, Lucien, moved out of the city they were both born in and now he lives two hours away. Before Lucien moved, Andy could arrive in minutes and still have daylight to spare, but now, for Andy to arrive at the party on time, he would have to leave when it is dark out.

And Andy absolutely cannot be outside at night.

'Please Andy, please!' Lucien begged on the other end of the phone.

'There's still time for you to get here. We can hold off ordering pizza too,'

'I'm sorry Lucien, I can't go,'

'Even after all that happened, she's still making things hell,'

'Who?'

'Your ex!'

'Oh,' Andy looked at the floor in his apartment as if it were a portal to his memories.

Last autumn, Andy dated a girl. In the spring of the year after, they broke up. Their romance started as a passionate adventure and ended putrid, sour, and cursed. She absorbed every piece of happiness in Andy's life until it festered, and since then, Andy has never left his house at night. He knows Lucien thinks the reason for this, is that Andy wants to cry all night, but that's only half true.

'Sorry, sorry,' Lucien squeaked on the other end of the phone.

'It's okay. You're completely right. But I promise you I'll make tonight up to you. Are you free anytime next week?'

'Yup, should be. Thursday maybe?'

'I'll take you out for lunch. Oh, and you can choose anything from AloneGalaxy, on me.'

'It's a deal. Have a nice night,'

'And you too, bud.'

The phone beeped as Lucien hung up. Andy put it on his coffee table and went to his balcony window. Wrapped in the darkness below was his car in its parking place, and there was one round, white spot on his bonnet: The moon. Andy forced his eyes to follow the path of the light, up to the moon in the sky, and then he glared at it. A few seconds later he realized that his lips were curled at one end.

'Fuck you.' He whispered as if he feared getting caught by it. Andy turned back around and went to the TV. Underneath it was a game console, which he switched on and picked up the controller. He sat back on the sofa and waited for his console to load. His eyes wandered around his living room as he waited for it to load.

On the coffee table were five plates and a brown banana peel. On a small table next to the sofa were seven glasses. He looked back up and his game had loaded. Hours passed as Andy screamed and swore down the mic, ferociously slamming the buttons on his controller. Eventually, he put it down and stood up to stretch. He picked up his phone off the coffee table and the time on the screen jumped at him: 3:00am.

After the breakup he felt he was playing games for longer hours each day; he had too much time on his hands. Andy considered going to bed, but the idea of being alone in bed where it was cold and too big repulsed him. Instead, he closed his eyes and concentrated on how to entertain himself next. When he opened them, he immediately looked at a drawer in his TV cabinet.

A tired Andy wobbled over to the draw and pulled it open. Inside, a wooden box was buried under unopened letters and old magazines. Picking up the box, he opened it and, pulled out half a cigarette of marijuana and a lighter in the shape of a cowboy hat. Despite his shaky hands, Andy managed to light the cigarette and began to smoke it. After a few minutes, he put the remainder of the cigarette back in the box and shut it.

It felt like an eternity for him to reach his sofa again, but when the feeling of sinking into his cushions caught up with him, he felt peaceful. His eyes moved to his balcony, at the darkness outside. He wished he could go for a night-time walk, but she would not let him. As soon as he'd stepped out the door, his head would begin to ache. Then his sight would go dim, and he'd throw up.

After Andy broke up with his girlfriend, she ruined his life, and he loathed her for it. She hangs in the night sky glowing down as if she is the queen of the twilight or a safe place in the darkness of night, but Andy knew she was quite the opposite of her beautiful reputation.

He could not tell anyone he dated The Moon, because no one would believe him. No one would comprehend that he met her when he was on a midnight walk when she appeared to him.

He was perched by the river near his apartment, pondering into its dark depth, wondering how cold it actually was, when a woman with silver hair sat next to him. She told him she was The Moon, and that she observes situations like his every night. Andy did not believe her until she glowed for him. Her skin radiated a gentle, silver glow, and the irises in her eyes were perfect images of a full moon.

Evening after evening, he spoke to her in the sky. She started to appear in human form more often as they grew closer. She enjoyed visiting his apartment, and going for midnight walks together. On one walk, she kissed him. Andy considered her his saviour, the beautiful woman that could care for him and save him as he kissed her back.

Lying on his sofa, Andy remembered they had taken photos together on their first date, and he slowly raised his phone to his face, and opened his photos app. He scrolled past all their other memories, determined to relive everything in chronological order until he reached the one he was looking for and Andy's consciousness entered the photo. He saw the events of the photo as if it were a movie:

The photo of a rugged, bearded man, next to an attractive young woman with silver hair, both of them grinning.

'I love it!' the woman chirped when she lowered Andy's phone from their faces and handed it back to him, 'Something to remember this day with.'

'Yeah,' Andy said.

They sat at an outside table and a restaurant, with flowers and candles in the centre of it. The Moon ate a spoonful of the soup in front of her.

'So, what are your hobbies?' She asked him.

'I play video games, and I collect records,' he responded.

'Records as in music?'

'Yeah,' Andy chewed the last slice of his steak.

They continued to eat in silence until The Moon said, 'I like to swim,' and Andy nodded in response.

Andy scrolled to another photo:

A woman lying in bed, half wrapped in the duvet. Her back, hair, and butt are visible.

Andy softly placed his phone on the bedside and crept into bed with the woman.

'I am awake, you know,' she said.

'Oh, sorry.' Andy felt his face warm up.

The woman rolled over and stared at him, smiling. Then she moved her hands onto his chest and pulled herself closer to him.

'Did you get a drink? That was quite the exercise,' she giggled.

Andy reached over to his bedside and picked up a glass of water.

'Here,' he handed it to her. 'Do you want anything else?'

'No, thanks. I am just going to go to the toilet though.' The Moon shuffled out of the bed and left the room. Andy grabbed his phone again and looked at the picture he took of her. He then opened his messaging app and went on his chat with Lucien and sent the photo.

The next photo Andy looked at was much further on in their relationship than the last one, and it took some scrolling to get to:

A woman in a silly hat and sunglass posing in the middle of a second-hand shop.

'I don't need this photo,' Andy whined.

'I know but I want to keep it and I don't have a phone. So, hold on to it for me, please,' The Moon smiled and removed the hat and glasses. When she returned them to their place, she noticed something across the shop, squealed, and ran over to it. It was a men's shirt, clearly many sizes too big for her.

'Isn't this amazing! I love the Alice blue colour,' She took it off the rack and held it up to show Andy.

He shrugged, 'I don't want to wear it.'

'Not for you, for me,' she huffed and trotted to the nearest mirror and positioned it to her shoulders.

'But it was in the men's section,' Andy reminded her.

The Moon frowned at him, 'That doesn't matter. It'll still look good with my jeans,'

'Put it back, you're embarrassing me,' Andy grabbed the shirt and lowered it from her shoulders.

The silver-haired woman became deflated. She turned around, marched to the rack the shirt was from, and hung it up.

'What's the matter? Why are you mad at me?' Andy seized her arm and jerked her to meet his eyes.

Andy felt his anger rise at the memory. She made him feel like a fool. He couldn't look at this photo anymore, so he scrolled to another. His finger landed on what he recognised to be the last photo he took with The Moon:

A mirror photo. A man in dirty joggers and a t-shirt, and a woman in jeans, a blouse, and a jacket, stand next to each other.

'We are going to be late,' Andy tightened his fist.

'I just thought a quick photo would be nice. To remember our first

Valentine's Day,' The Moon handed Andy's phone back to him and then bent down to tie her shoes.

'Oh, for fuck's sake!' he exclaimed.

'What?! I don't want to trip on the way out!' She finished tying, stood up, and gestured to herself, 'How do I look?'

'I hate it when you wear trousers.' Andy's face scrunched up after looking her up and down.

The Moon threw her arms out and grunted.

'Couldn't you wear a dress?'

The Moon spoke back with a shaky voice, 'Why do you hate me?'

'You're so stupid. I said hate the TROUSERS. Not YOU,' Andy stepped forwards and snatched her arm. The Moon stumbled forward, then used her other hand to shove Andy off.

'What the fuck? Don't you dare try and tell me that hurt,' Andy was staring fiercely at his sorrowful girlfriend.

'It did...' The Moon moved herself to the other end of the hall.

'Now you are making me seem like I'm abusive. Maybe I do hate you.' Andy snatched his key off the cabinet and unlocked the front door.

'Why? I've done nothing wrong; I tried to save you like you wanted me to!' The Moon yelled after him, 'What will make you like me? What more will I have to do?'

'You could start by wearing a dress. Me and Lucian, both agree you look hotter in a dress,'

'What does Lucian have to do with this?! Why would Lucien care if I look hot?'

'He thinks your nudes look hot,' Andy spat, and the room went quiet. Andy started, determined but he couldn't stop the embarrassment of revealing his own secret. The Moon's expression went cold and apathetic.

'I'm breaking up with you. I never want to see you again.' She walked towards the door. Andy stayed silent. Before stepping outside, The Moon turned around and pointed in his face.

'You'll never see me again either. In this form or the other. If you step outside at all in my presence, I will decimate you.' The Moon spun on her heels and left.

Andy put his phone down. Fear and hopelessness overwhelmed him after seeing the disturbing memory. He pushed himself off the sofa and stumbled to his balcony, then burst into tears.

'I hate you,' he snarled, as he unlocked the door. 'I should have hit you harder,' he said, pulling the doors wide open and clasping his hands on the railing.

'I want to kill you.' Andy's arms shook when he tried to hold the weight of his body on them. He awkwardly tipped his leg over the railing, and his shaking arms gave way.

The fall wounded him but didn't kill him. Instead, he lay still on the grass and let the moonlight beat down upon him.

# Platform Zero

---

## Emily Burton

# Platform Zero

When the announcement for the train came, my fiance Maddi and I were sitting in the deserted waiting room, deep in debate over whether turtles could snore. Over our heads, an old speaker droned.

*The train to Platform Zero has arrived.*

'I'm telling you,' I said, ignoring the announcement. ' At Daisy's yesterday, Timothy snored.'

'And I'm telling you, you were drunk. You're confused,' Maddi replied.

'Are you calling me mental?'

I glared at her. She giggled, pushing her golden hair over her shoulder. I couldn't help but smile as she slipped her arms around my waist. I bent down, kissed the top of her head, and squeezed her hand.

A gentle cough came from behind us. We turned to find a kind-faced old woman with eyes the colour of syrup.

'Sorry to interrupt, but could one of you hold my bag for a moment,' she said.

'Of course,' I smiled back at her. She opened her handbag, pulling out a tiny hairbrush, lipstick, and circular mirror. She handed me the bag, gazed into the mirror and smoothed down her wispy hair with the brush. With a shaky hand, she applied nude lipstick before stopping to admire her handiwork. She reminded me of my late grandmother, whom I had watched get ready so many times I'd committed the routine to memory.

'Thank you dear,' she said. I handed her bag back.

'You're welcome.' I grinned. 'You look lovely.'

As she replaced her belongings into the bag, her eyes twinkled at me.

'My husband's treating me to a holiday.'

'Adorable. How long have you guys been together?'

'Nearly sixty years.' She uttered these words like a child, every syllable oozed with giddiness and excitement.

'That's amazing,' Maddi leaned her head against my shoulder, and I kissed her forehead. 'We've been dating for three.'

'You look good together.'

She glanced at the announcement board; I followed suit. Its white lettering provided a stark contrast to the dark background. No other trains departed from the station.

'I better get going,' the woman continued, 'My legs don't work the way they used to.'

Maddi and I stood aside, allowing her to pass. She meandered down the corridor, rounded the corner and out of sight. I turned to my fiancé.

'I still think turtles can snore.'

## OLD WOMAN

So tired, yet so happy.

A cup of tea and a jam doughnut call my name as I make my way towards the platform. After a tiring, but lovely week with our daughter, I'm looking forward to reuniting with my husband. The dress he likes trails along the floor as I pat my hair.

*The train to Platform Zero will depart in three minutes.*

The corridor is long, but my legs are weary. I consider quickening my pace, but I don't want to push it. I need to be fighting fit for this trip. If I miss this train, it's not the end of the world. I can always get the next one.

## PENNY

We walked through the station, an unremarkable, stark building. The walls, along with everything else, were a wash of muted tones: creams, whites and light greys. The woman walked a little way ahead of us. A lump formed in my throat as another announcement came.

*All passengers must board the train at once. Leaving in one minute.*

'First to board gets to pick the movie tonight!' Maddi yelled. This got us moving. Maddi's taste in films left much to be desired. As we ran, the train screeched with impatience. I ran faster than Maddi. Having been a part of my uni's badminton team in the second and third, my stamina had improved. How could it not be with me darting across the court all game, every game? Maddi on the other hand avoided running whenever she could. We sprinted past the old woman towards the platform.

'Come on slowpoke, we're going to miss it,' I said. I glanced over my shoulder to see Maddi twelve feet behind me.

'I'm coming as quickly as I can.'

With flushed faces and chests feeling like they would collapse, we were fast approaching the train. I won, though Maddi wasn't too far behind. I shot a triumphant smile at her as she jogged up, her face red with effort.

'Guess we're watching Streetcar,' I grinned.

'Again?' Maddi shook her head and laughed. 'We only watched it the other day.'

'But Vivian Lee.'

A man stood by the train doors, welcoming us on board with a smile. A ticket box hung around his pale neck; the top half of his face covered by a giant conductor hat.

'You're just in time ladies.'

Grins spread across our faces like butter on bread. I turned to thank him, but he'd gone. The lump in my throat hardened as the train pulled away from the station. The old woman approached the platform. She stopped for a moment, her body heaving. I looked around for the train conductor.

'Sir!'

'Yes, ma'am?'

I jumped as he appeared out of the blue, before composing myself.

'There's a lady on the platform who missed the train. Can we go back? Her legs—'

'—We never go off schedule. No exceptions.'

I looked away for a split second. When I looked back, he'd disappeared. An announcement rang in our ears:

*The train to Platform Zero has departed.*

## OLD WOMAN

'Please, wait!'

My cries fall on deaf ears: the train puffs out of sight as I fade away.

## PENNY

I leaned against the train doors, pulling my phone from my pocket. Maddi stood opposite me as we tried to catch our breath.

'Right, I'm settling the turtle debate,' I said, waving my phone screen at her. She shook her head.

'Trusting Google over me? The betrayal!'

I wiped the air with my phone, sighed and put it away.

'No signal. Typical — we'll have to finish this later.'

I glanced out of the door again as Maddi wrapped her arms around me. The image of a happy couple reflected back at us. Outside, the world was nothing.

'We shouldn't be in a tunnel — we've only just left the station,' I said. Out of the corner of my eye, I could have sworn I saw Maddi's eyes flicker as we broke apart.

'Anyway.' Maddi took hold of my arm. 'Let's find our seats.'

She took out a pair of tickets from her pocket and examined them.

'Carriage A. I'm seat 1, you're seat 2.'

The tickets slipped out of her grasp. I bent to pick them up, but she stopped me, bending down herself. She stuffed them into her pockets and smiled.

'Let's go.'

We walked through a carriage where tragic faces wore tragic expressions. We made our way to the only other carriage on the train as grave-faced men in business suits looked artfully at one another, murmuring things that weren't quite audible. In the centre of the carriage, a woman cradled her baby wrapped in white blankets, its face angled away from onlookers. Its mother rocked back and forth in silence. I tried to approach her, and Maddi pulled me back.

'Leave her alone.'

'What do you mean?'

I turned to face her in confusion. She grabbed my arm and pulled me down the aisle and through the door separating the carriages. I yanked my arm free.

'What's all that about? Why're you acting weird?' I asked.

'I'm not being weird; I'm protecting you.' She planted a kiss on my forehead.

'I don't need protection.' I tried to sound cross and fight the smile forming on my face, but to no avail. We held hands walking into carriage A.

Four hard, white chairs were arranged in a square in the middle of the carriage, leaving the rest of the space empty. Each seat had a small place card with a number on it: one, two, three and four. Seats three and four were already occupied by a heavy-eyed man in army uniform, the other by an old man. Dressed in a knitted jumper and baggy trousers, he chatted away to the other man.

'So I said to her, look Doris, you may have fooled the others, but I know your type. I'm not lending you my woolly hat and that's that. As he finished, the other man chuckled.

'The nerve of some people.'

Noticeably quieter, the younger man chose his words carefully as if wary of who might overhear.

Both smiled at us as we took our seats.

'Hello,' said the younger man. 'What're your names?'

'I'm Penny, and this is my fiancé, Maddi,' I said. I glanced over at Maddi. She didn't look up from her phone. 'What's yours?' I asked him, nudging Maddi. She ignored me.

'Jack.'

We shook hands. Maddi gave him a tight-lipped smile before returning to her phone.

'And I'm Archie,' the old man butted in. We also shook hands. Maddi grimaced; I rolled my eyes.

'Don't mind her, she gets annoyed when I talk to strangers. She thinks I'm bothering people.'

'Hang on,' Maddi protested, 'you're making me sound horrible.' She laughed, and I laughed too.

'Nonsense, it's lovely to see a young person with spirit. My wife, though she's much older than you, is a firecracker herself. I'm meeting her at platform Zero — I can't wait to see her!'

'That's so sweet.'

Maddi leaned her head against my chest as the carriage fell quiet for a moment. The train chugged on a lullaby.

'Where're you headed?'

I glanced over in the direction of the voice and caught Archie's eye.

'Maddi booked us a weekend getaway in the mountains. I got accepted onto an internship in London, so this is a chance for us to spend quality time together before I go.' I kissed Maddi's cheek.

'That's adorable. Congratulations on the internship,' Archie grinned at me. 'What's it for?'

'A fashion magazine,' I beamed at him. 'Where're you guys off to?'

'As a matter of fact, I'm off to the mountains as well. And, so is Jack.'

'How do you two know each other?'

'Oh, we don't!' Archie laughed. 'We only met on this train. I'm talkative and Jack doesn't mind. As I said, I'm going on holiday with my wife.'

He pulled a photo out from his wallet and handed it to me. I knew that face; I knew those eyes. I handed it to Maddi, and for a split second sadness flickered in them. This left as soon as it arrived.

'We saw her. She missed the train I'm afraid.'
I handed the photo back to Archie. He gave it one last loving look before tucking it back into his wallet.

'What back luck! Never mind, I'm sure she'll get the next one.'

'How about you, Jack?' Maddi asked.

'I'm meeting my partner,' he blushed.

'That sounds lovely.' I smiled at him. 'How did everyone meet their partners? I love learning how people met.'

'Since you're asking,' Archie grinned.


## ARCHIE

'It was the first day of English O Level. Two students were in a fight: Joe Smith, the school bully, and Nell Edwards, the fiercest girl in school. Nobody wanted to get on the wrong side of her. It's safe to say she did not take kindly to being told to shut up and make a sandwich. The whole class egged them on as they tumbled to the floor. My friends and I made bets on who would win: all my money betted on Nell. Without warning, she kneed Joe in the privates and he went down like a sack of potatoes. Our teacher, Miss Nelson, wasn't too pleased when she entered the room. She called them both outside. They were both in BIG trouble. As they trailed back in, I tapped Nell on the shoulder and congratulated her on her fighting skills.'

'So let me get this straight: your wife beat a boy in her class up for misogynistic comments?' Jack said.

'Pretty much.' I grinned at everyone's facial expressions, amused at their admiration. Since they were enjoying my stories, I told them another. This one is set five years later, when Nell and I were married and living on a farm.

'It must have been a week before our wedding. I lay on the sofa, recovering from the previous night, drifting in and out of sleep, when I awoke by Nell shouting. I swear to God Archie get out here now she yelled. So naturally, I heaved myself up and stumbled out of the house and into the yard, half asleep and hungover. It had been quite a night: one minute I was talking to our neighbour over the fence about football scores, and the next singing at the top of my lungs in his kitchen with a beer in my hand.

Anyway, Nell appeared from inside the sty — she asked me why the pigs were all wrapped in blankets. The pigs trotted out behind her in an orderly fashion, each wearing different coloured blankets t trailing in the mud.

Nell wasn't impressed when I told her they were pigs in blankets.'

Penny had tears of laughter streaming down her face and a smile twitched on Maddi's lips. Across from them, Jack shook with laughter: they were quite the audience.

'You should have seen her face. I thought she was going to kill me right then and there,' I said.

'Now that is relationship goals,' Penny said, turning to Maddi. 'If we're not like that when we're older, I don't want it.'

Everything changed in a second. Tears of laughter turned to tears of grief.

'I've unlocked a new memory,' I said quietly. 'About last night:'

'The bathroom door stood ajar. I went to close it when I saw her lying on the floor, red seeping under her head. I called her name repeatedly, but she didn't answer. I checked her pulse. Almost non-existent.

I staggered down the stairs with her in my arms and carried her to the car. She became limp as I laid her on the back seat. There wasn't time to call an ambulance. We needed to go to the hospital at once.

I swerved left and right through the traffic as Nell deteriorated by the minute.

A scream of brakes, unimaginable pain, blurred faces, and voices as I lay in the middle of the road.

I died.

## JACK

The carriage fell into a stunned silence. Archie burst into tears. I leaned forward in my seat.

'You can't be dead; you're sitting right here.'

"It's what I remember.'

'That means we're dead too?'

'I guess,' Archie replied, his voice shaking. 'But where's Nell? Does this mean she survived?'

Maddi gave him a look telling him all he needed to know. He sobbed louder, burying his head in his hands.

Jack, do you have any memories?' Maddi asked. Penny looked at her, shocked.

'How are you not freaking out right now?'

I looked from one person to the next, bracing myself. 'I didn't think it had worked.'

'I'll always love you, remember that. That was the last text my boyfriend sent me before he took his own life. Everyone tells you it's okay to allow yourself to grieve. But no one warns you about the anger, the sheer resentment towards the deceased for leaving you behind. I'd had enough. I arranged the letters we'd written to one another in a circle and sat in the middle of it. In one hand I held a photo of us, in the other a razor.'

My voice faded away. I stared at the floor. No one spoke. Maddi glanced from one person to the next, a strange expression on her face.

## PENNY

The memory hit me hard. I jumped out of my seat, pointing an accusing finger at Maddi.

'I know what you did.'

'Sorry?' she said.

'We had an argument yesterday evening. I expressed my excitement about my internship in London, and you. When I asked you when you could visit, you were silent. You wouldn't even acknowledge me. I asked you why every time I brought London up you would give me silent treatment. You called me paranoid. I asked you if you were happy for me.

We've argued lots of times, but never have you gone off at me as you did last night. You called me selfish, I only wanted to go to London because you wouldn't be able to keep an eye on me. The accusations you threw at me stung. I yelled back, telling you to stop controlling my life and to be happy for me. Just this once.'

'Penny...' Maddi stood up and started towards me. I backed away. I shook like mad, holding back tears.

'We went for a drive later. To make up. I still felt uneasy about the screaming match we had a few hours before, but you seemed to want to fix things, so I trusted you. You made small talk in the car, asking me about the house I'd be renting and what I most looked forward to when I got to London. You drove until we reached the cliffs. You stopped the car, and we got out. You held my hand as you guided me toward the edge.

You apologised for the things you said. You told me you loved me, that nothing could separate us. You wrapped your arms around my body and kissed me. A thousand words were exchanged in a single kiss. And then, you pulled me over the edge.'

'Penny...'

'You're a murderer.'

The train slowed down. We had left the tunnel. A sign, polished and eerily perfect with 'Platform Zero' painted in bold greeted ust the station's entrance and where each door would arrive stood a shadowy figure.

'Why are we stopping?' I demanded. 'Have we arrived?'

'No,' Maddi mumbled. 'We can't be there yet.'

I glared at my fiancé as we sat back down.

'You knew this whole time!'

'I've been here before.' She refused to look at any of us.

A sign flashed above the carriage door. Its letters were bright, almost comical in their desperation to be seen by the passengers on board.

ALL PASSENGERS MUST CHECK THEIR TICKETS. IF YOUR TICKET HAS CHANGED, PLEASE MOVE TO YOUR NEW CARRIAGE. ASSESSMENTS HAVE TAKEN PLACE.

A flurry of movement appeared outside, businessmen from the other carriage stormed off the train. One of them spoke to a figure on the platform. The figure in question was featureless, hidden by a black cape and a hood. The men blatantly pointed in the direction of our carriage and their voices grew louder.

'I am a good man,' one of them said.

'Do you know who you're talking to?' another one chimed in.

'I demand to speak to the person behind this operation. It's a disgrace,' said the third man.

Their voices wrestled with one another for the guard's attention. One by one they begged, pleaded, and forced crocodile tears. One by one they were dismissed back to the other carriage, their heads hung low in defeat.

'Penny?'

'Leave me alone.' I turned away, staring out of the window at the figure outside. Its head turned in her direction. A face that wasn't a face.

'Penny!'

I reluctantly turned away from the window.

'What?'

'Here's your ticket.'

Maddi handed the small white rectangle over, glancing at her own. I took it.

'Mine's still the same,' I said.

Opposite us, Jack and Archie were examining their own tickets. They both nodded.

'Mine's also the same.'

'So is mine.'

Maddi couldn't take her eyes away from the tiny piece of paper. 'Mine's changed,' she said.

'Good,' I said. My eyes didn't leave the window. 'You can ruin someone else's afterlife.'

'But this is all wrong. It's not meant to end like this,' Maddi protested.

My hand shook, tracing the outline of the ring on my finger with the thumb on my other hand. An emerald ring, engraved in silver. We picked it out together the previous Christmas, the sample size a perfect fit. I slipped the ring off and handed it to her. She hesitated before taking it.

'Go,' I said.

The atmosphere remained heavy as Maddi left the carriage. None of us knew what to say, nobody knew how to feel. The hooded figure entered the carriage. It glided over to me, handing me something bundled in white blankets. As I took it, the baby from the other carriage stared back at me.

I rocked the baby as Jack and Archie watched.

'Tell us a story,' Archie whispered, his eyes red and sore. 'Anything. To let us forget.'

I looked down at the baby, who gazed back up at me.

'My grandmother always said I'd be an artist... She took me to my first ever art gallery.'

'Exquisite statues towered over me. Behind them, walls lined with paintings of every shape, size, and colour four-year-old me could think of. Flowers, people, places, and things brought the canvases to life, a thousand stories conveyed in each one, hundreds of ideas set off in my mind.

'Penny, where are you?'

I looked around. My grandmother came hurrying towards me. The smell of lavender perfume drew nearer as she approached me.

'There you are. Come along, it's time to go home.'

I didn't know I was crying until I could taste the salt. My eyeliner smudged and ran down my face as I wondered if I'd see her in the afterlife. A cracking noise, like the sound of something snapping in two, startled us. The carriage juddered forward. I turned around in my seat. The two carriages were no longer connected to one another. A vast, black nothingness replaced the corridor between the two carriages. Another announcement flashed up on the screen. The letters were even brighter this time.

CONGRATULATIONS. YOU HAVE PASSED THE ASSESSMENTS. TRAIN TO ARRIVE IN 15 MINUTES.

"Well, we made it." Jack smiled. Archie put his head in his hands once more.

I closed my eyes, holding the baby close to my chest.

Come along, it's time to go home.

I looked up into my grandmother's kind face. She took my hand in hers and squeezed it. Together, we walked towards the big exit doors.

I looked down at the baby, putting one of my hands on top of his, like Gran used to do with me.

Gran, I'm coming home.

# Lost Echoes

## Cayton Cameron

# Lost Echoes

*Awaken, young prince. The fires of war are all but burnt out; I have shielded you within the smoke, camouflaged from the foreign invaders. You are safe now, child, cocooned within the smoke, yet this moment of solace cannot last forever as I must release you once again unto the world outside. Use your gift to help you in this new world and walk ever in the shade but always look to the light.*

After being lowered to the ground by the smoke, a cold marble floor seemed to be all it took for the young prince to awaken from his deep slumber, the thick smoke dissipating as he regained consciousness. The prince slowly opened his eyes and was seemingly in no rush to stand up, instead lying on the hard floor examining the ceiling and all its intricate swirls and designs not entirely faded from the passing of time.

The prince raised a hand to his face, twisting and turning it, brushing his skin with his other hand, unsure if he was in a dream or had finally awoken. His surroundings seemed familiar yet foreign, as if in a distorted fantasy rather than reality. Sitting upright took a surprisingly monumental effort, his muscles and bones creaking from their lack of use over time.

A cold wind blew past the tattered curtains blowing away the blanket previously draped over the prince's shoulders and sending a chill through him as proof of his consciousness. His eyes darted to the blackened curtains swaying in the wind before the huge windows; what remained of the glass failed to repel the outside elements.

Rays of light shone through the rips in the curtains, burning the boy's weakened retinas as he rose from the floor. His eyes had felt unusually sensitive since his reawakening, causing him to recoil in pain from the brightness. The boy shivered as he once again felt the cold air hit his skin; his tattered shirt and ripped trousers offered little protection against the cold. Remembering the blanket that had been draped over his shoulders, he scanned the charred floor noticing it near one of the windows. The boy stared out of the window as he approached the blanket and picked it up in one hand, his gaze unmoving as he attempted to discern what lay outside. While at a distance, he noticed what lay beyond seemed unusually blurry, and even as he closed the gap, the scenery outside the window seemed just as blurry as before.

Brushing the ruined curtain aside so he could see the entire window, the boy pressed his face as close to the glass as he could and yet only saw blue and green shapes outside. The boy imagined the view instead from memory. He imagined peering out of the window and taking in the scenery of the great plains before him; he had rarely set eyes upon a view that could compare; it was so grand and yet so comforting. The sun would gently caress the lush greenery, and he would always spot the subtle amber tips on the grass. Letting his father know autumn was nearing, was his unofficial role as royal watchman.

His eyesight was worsening, and the thought of never being able to look upon the place where he spent his childhood and reminisce was a possibility that terrified him. As his fingers gently traced the edges of the broken glass still attached to the window frame, a voice called out to him.

*Come here, young prince.*

The boy quickly jolted around, scanning the chamber repeatedly before seeing a brief glimpse of what looked like a spectral figure walking towards one of the hallways. Uncertain of if he had really seen the figure, he debated following it, though he was too curious to miss out on the possibility of adventure and discovery. As he walked towards the hallway, he stopped at the centre of the room, noting a spotless circle of the floor, the shiny marble contrasting with the worn-down appearance of the rest of the room. This was where he had awoken; the two strands of golden light that had gone directly into his retinas just earlier still remained centring on that one spot. He thought that maybe he really did have a guardian spirit; maybe his grandfather's stories weren't as fictional as they seemed. Though with no way of proving it wasn't a coincidence, he could not be certain.

The air was warm around the palace, the cold breeze from before having disappeared almost entirely, the boy would have abandoned his blanket were he not using it as a cloak to hide his damaged clothes. On days like these, the prince would swim in the nearby river on the north side of the palace for hours until the sun went down. Though his father hadn't allowed him to leave without a small detachment of guards after an incident where swimming too close to a fast-running stream had almost ended his life. Yet he still enjoyed visits to the river, nevertheless. Back then, he had no concern for danger, despite the many times he had been warned.

The noises of nature were absent now; the usual birdsong, croaking of frogs and even howling of distant wolves had disappeared; the palace had never been so uncomfortably silent before. On even the quietest days, there were still the servants and maids who would usually be busy enough to hear the constant clicking of heels on the marble floor could be heard throughout the day.

*A gift from the past waits for you in the hallway, young prince.*

He was sure he had heard the voice again though wasn't sure exactly where it came from, its comforting voice almost compelled him to listen. As the boy ventured through the long hallway, he noticed something lying on the floor in the middle of the room; unable to see its exact shape or features, he approached. Nearing the object, it appeared to be a crown, though the only one he ever saw had belonged to his father. The unusual placement of the crown did not concern the boy, though he was overcome with curiosity the moment he saw it.

Frustrated at his inability to define its details, the boy kneeled to examine the crown more closely. He noticed how similar it was to the one his father wore, due to the specific choice of gems within it and its lightweight appearance unlike the crowns belonging to the rulers of nearby kingdoms. A large shining sapphire adorned the front of the headpiece, a distinctive symbol of the family's royalty and long reign; on either side of the jewel was a small emerald, a gem rarely found outside the kingdom's borders. The boy's grandfather often recited the meaning behind the jewel's inclusion within the crown, having witnessed its creation alongside his father. The jewels embedded in a crown often directly related to the ruling family and their fortunes; the larger gem was considered a major influence, while the smaller gems were a minor influence. In that crown, the minor influences were safety, wealth, and nature, while the major influences were tranquillity, longevity, and a close connection with guardian spirits.

A legacy spanning four generations and over a hundred years lay before him in the form of his father's crown, the boy felt both a sense of intrigue and intimidation from standing in its presence. An aura of power emanated from it, glistening in the sun as rays of light bounced off it and illuminated the gems as they began to emit a faint glow; the scene seemed almost holy yet suspicious.

The young prince reached for the crown, grasping it from the sides near the bottom to ensure no smudges or fingerprints were left upon it. Then, noticing its surprising weight despite its lightweight appearance, he ran his hands along the edges feeling the cold silver rim on his fingertips. The boy's grandfather would often mention the weight was due to the power from the sapphire on the front of the crown, as if it was the weight of the guardian spirits themselves as they influenced it.

Lifting the crown above his head, the prince slowly lowered it, almost afraid of the responsibility that came with it. But just before placing it on his head, he decided against it and held it in his hands as he thought of his father. He thought of where he might be and when he would be reunited with him. He thought of how much power the crown held, and how it would react when placed on the head of a boy rather than a man.

*A noble decision, though I implore you, touch but the sapphire on your father's crown and feel a fraction of its power. Feel the spirits of those from years past as they dance and they flitter around you.*

The boy refused to wear his father's crown as it was a responsibility he felt he was not ready for, yet he felt compelled to touch the sapphire adorned upon it. Hesitantly guiding his finger to the stone, he gently brushed it, feeling its smooth texture as his hearing suddenly hyper-focused on the sound, hearing the skin on his fingertip carefully grate upon it.

*Do you see them?*

The prince looked up from the crown as countless disembodied whispers flew past his ears; various voices of men, women and children floated around his head as if trying to get his attention without speaking directly to him. The voices spoke a familiar language, though with muffled voices and broken sentences. It was like walking through a crowded marketplace, overhearing small parts of conversations yet not fully taking in any of them.

*He is there too. Find him, young prince.*

Trying to understand what was happening, the boy was caught off-guard by a sudden flash of numerous spirits roaming throughout the hallway, appearing in the shaded parts of the room before quickly dissipating. He stumbled backwards in shock, almost dropping the crown as he fell upon the soft carpet. Scanning the room crowded with phantoms as he watched them look down at him and continue to converse with each other.

The boy smiled at one of the spirits before taking his finger off the sapphire, and in an instant, both the voices and spirits disappeared, leaving the palace once again in sombre silence as the sun began to set above the great plains. However, the boy would not watch this sunset as he always had, instead simply gazing upon the crown in wonder, realising that in that moment of vision gained from the stone, he had finally found his father.

# Sacrifice Is Mandatory

## Joshua Kevin Carr

# Sacrifice Is Mandatory

He's sitting low in the chair, leaning over the table, looking across at it. The creature is motionless and hidden in the darkness. Only its hands are visible, laid flat against the carved wood table. He waits, wipes the sweat from his brow. The light above them, a single bare bulb held by a cord to some unseen ceiling, reflects off his head. He is a stocky man, shorter than might be expected for someone with his build and with a creased face plastered to a balding head. He looks around; the light barely touches the ends of the table, giving him no way to gauge the size of the room. He looks at the hands, then again at the darkness, and comes to a resolution. He turns away from the table and braces himself to stand.

'Do not stand,' the voice says.

The man nods and turns back to face the voice. He stares at the darkness opposite him; there is almost a silhouette but it's impossible to tell against the void. The hands remain unmoving on the table. He looks at them and blinks, checking his vision. They are large and rough but something about the colour is off. They have a kind of sickly, blue-grey hue. They look like the hands of a man out in the cold, when all the blood has been diverted to his core. He places his hands together, under his chin, and looks at where he thinks the creature's eyes should be.

'So.' He stops, coughs into his hand, then continues, 'I'm guessing we're not just gonna sit around here all day, or night, and do nothing, are we?'

'No. Please excuse me for one moment.'

The hands move back, into the darkness, then push six stacks of playing cards onto the table. The man pulls his chair closer. He watches as the hands organise the cards into three pairs, checking the top card of each pile.

'We will play a game, using these cards,' the voice says.

'Uh-huh,' he says. 'A game. Right then, what game do you wanna play? I'm pretty good at blackjack myself.'

'I have created a game for us to play. You will need to pick one of the three pairs of decks.'

The hands push the cards to the man's side of the table. He examines the backs of the cards. They are different to any he has seen before. Instead of the standard red or blue back criss-crossed with white lines, these cards are marked in black ink. A simple design of fanged jaws closing around a shattered bone adorns them. The cards themselves are also different, being a light brown colour and specked with darker tones, not pure white paper. He looks closer at them. They look entirely hand crafted.

'Damn, you make all these yourself? They're quite something, huh.'

'Yes, I made them for this occasion. I am glad you find them pleasing,' the voice says. The hands remain fixed on the table.

The man sits up straight. He looks at the decks. A thought occurs to him and his eyes narrow, fixing on where the creature's eyes must be.

'Right. You made this game, the cards I mean, and, well, I assume, the rules too. You could've marked each card. So, how do I know that you'll play fair?'

'A valid objection. I give you my word, there would be no satisfaction in winning through a means beyond my own ability. As a show of good faith, I will allow you to choose the deck I play with, after you select your own,' the voice says.

The man nods, looks back at the cards. The cards do not have any of the signature dents, folds or scratches that he has seen con men use to dupe fools in the past. He licks his lips. With no information about the game or the cards, it is a totally random choice. He raises a hand, hovers it over the middle deck. He opens his mouth, squints. Another idea comes to him. Whatever this creature is, it listens to reason, he thinks. He drops his hand on the table.

'Now, I've gotta choose both my cards and yours... but I don't know what the differences between these cards are... so how can I make that choice?'

He looks into the darkness. The voice says nothing. He leans back in his chair, waiting.

'Another reasonable complaint. I will allow you to turn over the top card of one deck, to aid you in this decision,' the voice says and it raises a hand over the cards. 'When you are ready.'

The man strokes his chin and takes a deep breath. He is not a betting man, he thinks, as he eyes his options. He raises a finger and tilts his head. Perhaps, there is something else he needs to know before he can make this decision.

'Right, I got one more question for you, then I'll pick a card. We're gonna play this game of yours and you say you'll play fair, which I'm not saying I don't believe but... when I play a game with someone, I like to know the stakes first. So, what're we playing for.'

'A fair question. The stakes are simple: if you win, I will grant you one request,' the voice says, as it raises a hand then lowers it, raising the other. 'If I win, I will kill you.'

'That's pretty heavy. What if I don't wanna play with those stakes?'

'Then I will kill you now.'

The man stares at the creature. He tilts his head and wonders if it is sincere. It has been nothing but straight forward and seems to be utterly humourless. He lowers his head, wipes his brow; those really are the stakes. His eyes move across the cards. He places a hand on the left deck.

'Right. Right, those are the stakes. This is the deck I wanna see,' he says.

The creature moves a hand over the deck, places a finger under the card, another on top. It turns the card over and retracts its hand. The man looks across the card, taking in each detail. In the top left is a name, written in thick capitals: **HAMMERHEAD**. Beneath this name is a box with a jagged line drawn through it and smaller, pointed lines underneath. Water, perhaps? The top right features an icon of meat on a bone and the number 4. The centre of the card is decorated with a stylised drawing of a shark swimming, mouth agape and below that is an icon of fangs around the number 4 and a heart containing the number 3.

'The elusive **HAMMERHEAD**. It is a powerful oceanic predator. See the waves below the name? This deck contains creatures of the ocean's deep,' the voice says, as it turns the card face down, 'now you have seen a card, what deck do you choose?'

The man looks at the left pile. The card stays in his mind. He guesses how this game might be played. He looks at it and the decks. He winces and places a hand on the left deck.

'I can't lie, I don't like making this choice without knowing how to play but... I'll take this ocean deck.'

'Very well, now please choose my deck.'

The man looks at the remaining two pairs. He taps the table next to the rightmost deck and nods at the creature. It drags the middle cards into the darkness. The hands take his cards and place them on his side of the table. He stares at them. The table has small boarders cut into it, a little larger than the cards themselves. A pair of spaces sit on the right, occupied by his decks. In the middle are four more spaces on his side and a line runs down the middle of the table. The same markings are mirrored across the table, in front of the creature. He runs a finger along the cuts; had he not noticed them before? Or were they not there before? He hadn't paid the table much mind. He was shaken from this thought by the creature's voice.

'The deck on your furthest right contains copies of a single, weak creature. Please, draw one.'

The man looks at the deck and at the creature. His hand moves over the top card and its hand mimics. They draw a card. **FLOUNDER, 0** meat, **0** fangs, **2** hearts.

'Your creature is the feeble **FLOUNDER**. A pitiful fish that swims the seafloor and occupies the bottom of the food chain. It has no attack, only two health, but it can be played without any cost. There lies the use of this weak creature. The health, the hearts, are consumed as meat by greater creatures. Feed them and they will join you. That is how this game is played.'

'So, the other deck has all the big fish, huh?'

'That is correct. Please, draw three cards from it. That will be your opening hand,' the voice says as it takes the top cards of its own deck.

The man looks at his cards and thinks. He knows the top card is the **HAMMERHEAD** he saw before. He could either draw the **HAMMERHEAD** and two other cards or, as is customary, shuffle the deck before drawing. Knowing one of his cards could give him an advantage. His life is at stake; it would be good to have any upper hand given that the creature knows the game inside out. But it would be dishonest. He takes the deck in his hands and shuffles. He has never relied on trickery before, he will not start now.

'Now, you've said this game is fair. So, fair's fair. I don't know what I'm getting,' he says as he takes the top card. He turns it over: **LOBSTER, 2** cost, **1** attack, **3** health.

He draws another: **SWORDFISH, 3** cost, **3** attack, **2** health. Low-cost cards, good to start with.

He draws a final card: **KILLER WHALE**, 6 cost, 6 attack, 6 health. An apex predator. Not something he can play on the first turn. Still, it will be helpful later. A strategy is forming. It's always good to have a plan, he thinks.

'Now you have a starting hand, we can begin. Would you like to take the first turn?'

'Hmm...'

The first turn. The order of play, even between two people, can make all the difference.

'No, no. You go first. It's your game, you can show me how to play,' he says, gesturing to the creature's side of the table. He lays his cards down and places both hands under his chin.

'As you wish. I play my **IMP**,' the voice says, placing a card in the outer-left space. **0, 0, 2.**

'So, that's your freebie then, huh? My deck's all ocean themed, so what's this one?'

'Beings of the underworld; the demonic deck. I sacrifice both health from my **IMP** to play my **HELL HOUND**.'

It takes the **IMP** and places it back into the second deck, then puts the new card in its place. **2, 2, 2.**

'Ah, demons. So, what was the third deck?'

'Beasts of the forests and prairies,' the voice says. 'Oh, I have forgotten something.'

A hand retracts into the dark. It re-appears a moment later clutching a bowl of wooden disks, no bigger than poker chips.

'These tokens represent health. We place them on the creatures fighting for us so we may record their wellbeing,' the voice says, putting two chips on the **HELL HOUND**.

'Right. So, there were three decks, ocean creatures, forest creatures and... demons. Isn't that last one a bit different? I'd get birds, maybe. Water, land, air. But demons... I dunno, just seems out of place to me,' he says.

'I do not think they are out of place here,' the voice says.

He stares at the **HELL HOUND**. Maybe this thing just thinks they are interesting; they are certainly different from the others, he thinks. But...

'That is the end of my turn. You may begin yours now.'

The man picks up his cards. He moves a hand towards his decks.

'Which one do I draw from?'

'You do not draw on your first turn. You draw one card from each deck from then on.'

'Oh, that's... unique. Never played a game like this before. So, these are what I have to work with, huh?'

He surveys his cards. From watching the creature, he knows how to play but not how to win. He could play the **FLOUNDER**, then sacrifice it to play the **LOBSTER** but that would not be enough. Perhaps, he should play the long game...

'So, to win this game, I've gotta use my critters to kill yours and then...' The man waves a hand. He looks at the creature and shrugs, 'then, I win?'

'In a sense. At the end of a player's turn, their creatures attack, dealing damage equal to their attack value to the creature opposite them. If nothing opposes it, then a creature will strike the opponent directly. Five direct strikes is a victory.'

'Right,' he says. He looks at his cards again. He thinks, he can either block the **HELL HOUND** or trade direct hits. Another thought comes to mind. 'I didn't draw cos it was my first turn so, I'm guessing I can't attack on it either?'

'That is correct. The first draw and first attack will be on my next turn. Did I not say this? My apologies,' the voice says. The man flicks a hand and gives a smile. The voice is soothing and genuine. He nods to himself. If nothing else, this creature is totally sincere in all that it says.

'Ok then, I'll pass. Go ahead.'

'Are you sure?'

'Oh, yeah, sure enough. You take your turn,' he says. He places his cards down and leans back.

The hands do not move.

'Interesting. This is a... calculated risk, as I understand? You must have a plan you are confident in. Still, if that is your choice then I shall play.'

The creature picks up its cards and draws; the man watches it re-arrange them. It will probably get to attack him twice this turn. He will have some catching up to do but, with a little luck and some careful thought, he can win this, he thinks.

'I play my **IMP**,' the voice says, placing the card on the far right and two chips on it, 'then I sacrifice one health from both it and my **HELL HOUND** to play my **GLUTTINOUS FIEND**.'

The creature takes a chip from both its cards and places the **GLUTTINOUS FIEND** in the middle-left space. The man leans forward: **2, 0, 4**. This must be the start of a big move, six health on the board. Enough to play something really strong.

'I sacrifice all four health from **GLUTTINOUS FIEND** to play my **TERROR DEMON**,' the voice says, as it places down the new card: **4, 4, 2**. The visage of a horned, snarling face looks up at the man from the card.

'Ah, good play. You know, I can't deny, you've made a pretty nice game here,' he says, meeting where he thinks creature's eyeline is. 'I mean, these've got a style. I could definitely see people buying this.'

'They are not for sale,' the voice says, removing the **GLUTTINOUS FIEND** from the table, 'I end my turn. Both my **HELL HOUND** and **TERROR DEMON** attack you.'

It slides the cards forward. The man's legs go numb. His eyes widen; he cannot breathe. He touches his calf; it is cold. It slides the cards back to their places. He feels blood pump through his legs and takes a deep breath.

'What the hell was that! What'd you just do!'

'I attacked twice, two of five gone,' the voice says. It puts its hands together, 'Did I not mention this before?'

The man wipes his brow and takes another breath. He has got to be calm; he can win this if he thinks things through.

'What–what did you not mention before?'

The creature holds up a hand and stretches its fingers out wide.

'There is a reason it takes five strikes to win. One for each limb: legs, arms and finally... head,' the voice says, as it closes the hand into a fist and places it on the table.

'So, you mean that that'll happen again each time I get hit?'

'That is correct. It is your turn now.'

It points to his cards then places both hands flat on the table. The man looks at the creature; he looks at its hands, then at his own cards. He rubs his hands together and leans back. The way to win is to out manage your opponent, he thinks. The creature only has one card in its hand, so if he can kill the cards on the board, it won't be able to mount a comeback. All he has to do is draw something good and think things through. Play it calm, play it well, he mouths. A card from each pile. **FLOUNDER, KING CRAB: 1, 2, 1.** He nods.

'Right, gimmie just a minute to think this through,' he says as he arranges his cards. He runs through the moves he can make. These cards can block most of the creature's cards; they can kill some too. He smiles and licks his lips.

'Of course, take all the time you need. I must say, you are very... different... to how I imagined.'

The man frowns and looks up at the creature. He puts his cards down.

'What d'ya mean?'

The voice stays silent. The man looks around at the darkness. He drums his fingers on the table. It lifts its hands, sweeps them across the table, places one at each end.

'I must confess, I had my doubts as to whether you would agree to play this game with me. I am pleased you have taken my offer; I have thought a lot about this meeting.'

Something in the voice has changed, there is almost... joy. The man shuffles in his chair. He tilts his head and shrugs; this thing has been honest with him, might as well be honest with it.

'Not like you gave me much of a choice, waking up in here, told to play or die.'

The hands come together.

'There is always a choice.'

The joy is gone.

The man considers this. It did give him a choice, not a fair one but, still, a choice. That cannot be denied. But there was something in the tone. Even though the creature is hidden in the dark, just a pair of hands extended out, he could almost picture a face now.

'You have chosen to play and I am distracting you. I apologise. Please continue with your turn.'

He blinks and picks up his cards. Is it trying to get in his head? This could all be an act to throw him off...

No, he thinks. This creature wants to beat him, wants to show it is better than him. It wants him to play, so that is what he will do.

'Right, I play both of my **FLOUNDERS**,' he says as he places a card down on each end of the table. A hand puts two chips on each of his cards.

A smile emerges as his eyes move between his cards and the table, 'Now, I sacrifice both health from my right **FLOUNDER** and one health from my left one to play my **SWORDFISH**.'

The creature removes the chips as the man takes the deceased **FLOUNDER** back into his deck. He places the **SWORDFISH** in the middle left space. He takes the last chip off his right **FLOUNDER** and puts it back into the deck.

'I'll also play my **KING CRAB**.'

He places the card on the far left of the table. It places a chip on the card.

'I see your plan has borne fruit,' the voice says.

'Sometimes risks are worth taking,' he says. He slides his cards forwards. The hands remove the **HELL HOUND** and **TERROR DEMON** from the table.

'See, I think I've got this all down now.'

The man laughs and licks his lips.

'An impressive strategy.'

'You bet'cha,' he says as he puts down his cards, 'now, I think it's your turn.'

'Very well,' the voice says as it draws, 'I play my **IMP**, then I sacrifice it to play my **IMP TAMER**.' It places the card in the far left space: **2, 1, 3**. The drawing depicts a demon striking out with a thorned whip, its eyes ablaze.

'Now, I sacrifice one health from my **IMP TAMER** and the last health of my remaining **IMP** to play my **HELL HOUND**,' the voice says and places a card on the far right. 'Both my cards attack.'

It slides both cards forward. The man's right arm goes numb. He gasps. It pulls the cards back and the man takes the **KING CRAB** off the table.

'You only have two hits left.'

The man rubs his arm.

'Yeah...'

The creature watches him as he raises his cards.

'Strange, you are quite calm given the situation.'

He sighs and wipes an eye.

'Yeah, well, if you worked where I do, you'd be used to stress too.'

A hand taps the table.

'Your work is stressful?'

The man looks up.

'Huh, yeah. I'll tell you, those idiots've got no idea. I'm always running around putting out their fires. I mean this latest site, it's, well...' He sweeps his arms out wide, closes his eyes and shakes his head. 'It's a real mess. I mean wrong permits, accidents, everything done poorly and, uh, now I gotta deal with it,' he says. He tilts his head. 'Or not, I guess. I'm here. Someone else's problem now.'

The voice remains silent. The man waits a moment then picks up his cards again. He draws, **FLOUNDER**, **HAMMERHEAD**. He smiles.

'Okay, I play my **FLOUNDER**, then I sacrifice it to play my **LOBSTER**,' he says as he places the card in the far left, 'I'll also take one health from my **SWORDFISH** and all three from my **LOBSTER** to play this.'

The man takes the **LOBSTER** and puts the **HAMMERHEAD** in its place.

'Right, that about does it, my creatures attack,' he says and pushes the cards forward. A hand takes the **IMP TAMER** off the table.

'You land your first strike on me. Well done,' the voice says, picks up its cards. 'I will take my turn now.'

The creature draws, puts down its cards and places both hands on the table. The man stares into the darkness; he tilts his head up and blinks. What is it planning?

'I pass. My demon attacks you directly.'

The man shakes his head. He leans forward.

'You sure? I mean... ok, if that's what you're gonna do, then.'

'It is, I doubt you can win this now,' the voice says. It slides the **HELL HOUND** forward. The man grips his left arm; he cannot move it. The creature pulls the card back.

'One strike left to make. A moment, if you please.'

A hand vanishes into the darkness. The man rubs his elbow, makes a fist and then opens it. He still feels cold. The hand re-emerges. A curved blade sits in its palm.

'Hey, hey I–I still got a hit left, now.'

'I am aware,' the voice says as it places down the knife. 'I would like to offer you another choice. It looks as though you will lose this game. You can choose to fight on or... you can accept defeat now and I will grant you a quick and painless death.'

The hand moves back over its cards, leaving the knife in the middle of the table. The man looks at the semi-circular edge. He follows it down to the handle, a dark wood, imperfect finish. He scratches his chin. This thing has a point, he thinks. To catch up now would take a very lucky draw. He reaches out a hand, a finger, and runs it along the metal surface. His eyes widen and he pulls back.

'No. No, I ain't backing out. If you beat me, you beat me, but I go down on my own terms damn it. You're not getting to me that easy, understand?'

The creature does not move.

He swallows. Maybe it is getting to him. Just stay calm.

'Very well, though perhaps you will change your mind once you have drawn. I will leave it there for now.'

'I'd rather you didn't,' he says. He takes a glance at the knife and leans on his hand, covering his eyes.

'You may want to take my offer after you draw. It is your turn now.'

The man's hand moves over his decks. He looks at them and takes a deep breath. This is it. He draws his final cards: **FLOUNDER, MINNOW SHOAL. 3, 1, 6.** He stares at the cards, a smile moves across his face. The creature watches in silence. The man laughs. He looks it right where the eyes should be and nods to the knife.

'You wish to concede?'

He stops his laughter and simply smiles.

'No, I want you to know, you won't be needing that,' he says. 'I'll play my **FLOUNDER**, then I take two health from it and one from my **HAMMERHEAD** to play my **MINNOW SHOAL**.'

He places the card in the middle right space. The creature places six chips on the card. The man holds up a hand, takes five of those chips off the card and one off the **HAMMERHEAD**.

'I wasn't done just yet,' he says as he holds up the last card in his hand, 'you see this card, here? I've had it the whole game... and guess what.'

He places the **KILLER WHALE** in the far right space. The creature closes its hands.

'That's right, I'm playing it. Now, my creatures attack and that's your puppy gone and three hits on you. So, now we're even.'

'You are correct. It seems I have underestimated your luck. I will take my turn now,' the voice says as it takes a card from each deck. It moves the cards in its hand. The man waits for the creature to make a move but it stays still. He might just have got this, he thinks. At last, the voice says, 'Well played.'

It places its cards on the table and fans them out. The man looks into the darkness, looks at the cards.

**IMP: 0, 0, 2.**

**IMP: 0, 0, 2.**

**TERROR DEMON: 4, 4, 2.**

**OVERPOWER OVERLORD: 6, 11, 1.**

'I don't understand, what're you saying here?'

'You have won. No matter which cards I play, you will land a killing blow on me next turn. I pass.'

He stares at the creature.

'For real, you're not gonna play anything?'

It turns over both hands.

'What purpose could my moves have? You have won. Please take your victory turn.'

The man holds a hand over his cards. He puts a finger on the top card and stops. He looks into the darkness; the silhouette remains unmoving. He sighs and shakes his head.

'I don't need to take a victory turn. You played fair, so... I'll play nice, let's just say I won, shake on it and move on, eh?'

The man holds out a hand across the middle of the table.

The creature considers this. A hand meets his.

'Your actions surprise me. You played well, now name your request...'

# Invaders of Earth

## Ezra Chiu

# Invaders of Earth

An astronaut landed in the Forest Area today. Well, his spaceship did – right next to the gate. The orange paint was chipped on all four sides, but it looked like tiger stripes, so I don't think he'd mind too much. I looked for him the whole of lunchtime. Mrs. Key told me not to worry; she said she would get rid of *the box* when she could. I wanted to punch her. That's the astronaut's *stuff*!

I told Mum about it as soon as I got home.

'A box!' she said. 'Who would want to live in a box?'

I knew she wouldn't understand. That's okay. That night, I packed two char sui for lunch. I don't think I've ever been *that* hungry, but I thought Mr. Astronaut might be.

Sometimes, when Mrs. Key asks why I shovel rice into my mouth – when I could just use a spoon – I don't know what to say. Bao are a good compromise; almost a sandwich. If anybody asks me what I'm having for lunch, I'd just say *I'm eating a sandwich* – nobody throws sandwiches down the slide because they 'smell funky' and 'look like raw bacon'. I didn't think the astronaut would mind though. Rice and bread are both space-friendly.

I sat under the tree, beside the spaceship, and ate char sui bao. *I wonder what kind of guy you are, Mr Astronaut.* I thought about what I would say to him if I ever met him. Mum and Dad call me shy. I just think there's nobody here worth talking to.

'Hello, Mr. Alien! My name is Mei and I like anime. They're much cooler than cartoons. They're never too *girly*.'

I thought about him in maths class, too. The word 'polygon' belongs next to a spaceship, so I drew a little planet to prove it. The other girls talked about their future husbands. Charlotte told us Toby was *so cool* for kicking the football on the roof. I have always wanted to kick Toby in the face – his cheeks are squidgy. I'd like to see him squirm.

'What about you? Tell me who you have a crush on!' said Charlotte, from across the table. I ignored her.

'Come on!' Charlotte threw a rubber at me. 'Why are you so stuck up?'

'I don't like anyone.'

'Why not? Someone will think you're okay.' She smiled.

I looked at her and screamed.

Mrs. Key told Mum I had a hard day when she picked me up from school. Mum yelled at me for making a scene.

'Is this who you want people to think you are?' Mum said. She dragged me away. Mrs. Key didn't say anything.

That night, I locked myself in my room. I hung my blankets up and scattered satsuma peels across the floor – orange like the spaceship. *When will you come back, Mr Astronaut?*

He'd fly over and see me waiting for him with a packed lunch – he'll be so impressed, he'll teach me how to fly his ship.

'You see, alien technology lets us travel through time,' he'd say. 'Do you want to see the pyramids? Do you want Mum to tell you about fat ghosts and mountain cats again?'

'No, that's okay, I'd say, 'I have enough stories for both of us.'

I fell asleep waiting for him to turn up. On Monday and Tuesday, I wrote letters to him. I drew pictures of our schemes. He'd have long, black hair – just like me. Only, his skin would be lighter, and his eyes would be big enough.

On Wednesday, Mrs. Key called us together for Circle Time.

'Tomorrow, we will have a new member of our class,' she said. 'He's had a long trip –he'll be nervous, so we all want to try out best to make him feel welcome.'

I knew my letters worked then. Mr. Astronaut was coming back! He could sit next to me in maths and English. I don't think there's school in space, so his grammar might be a little rusty. I'll let him copy me. That night, I wrote one final letter:

*Dear Mr. Astronaut,*

*I can't wait to finally meet you! I'll make sure to come to school extra early. Do you like salty food or sweet food? I'll pack both, just in case. Tomorrow, I'll show you where your spaceship crashed. I looked after it, I promise!*

*If you're not too tired, we can fly to Mars. There's so much to do! Let's sleep well tonight.*

*Yours Sincerely,*

*Mei Yao.*


I folded the letter up put it in my lunchbox. I snuck two extra bao from the steamer and put them next to it. Mum wouldn't mind – she was still at work. I like to practice being sneaky, though. It's an important skill for an astronaut to have.

I woke up at 6am the next day. Nobody was at school when I got there. I sat outside the classroom until the bell rang.

'Mei,' said Mrs. Key, when she entered. She was holding a boy's hand. He looked just like my drawings – his straight, black hair ran down to his shoulders and he smiled wonkily at me. Only, in my drawings, he looked so brave.

'This is Stephen.'

'Oh,' I said. 'Hi.'

He didn't respond.

'Don't worry,' she said. 'I'm sure you'll have something to talk about.'

Stephen sat next to me in science and French. I ignored him in science. I figured I would have something to say to him by French.

'Why is your name Stephen?' I asked, instead of *Ça va?* (I didn't really care how he was).

'What?'

'Why is your name Stephen? It's a stupid name.'

'I don't think it's stupid.'

'It's boring,' I said, 'What happened to your Chinese name?'

'I have a Chinese name,' he said. 'I prefer Stephen.'

'How can anyone prefer *Stephen*?'

We didn't say anything to each other after that. The bell rang for lunch, and I grabbed his hand. We ran to his spaceship together.

'Look,' I said. 'I kept it safe for you.'

Stephen didn't respond.

'I know it's a bit rusty, but I think it looks cool – like a tiger. Are you sad because it's rusty? It'll be good when we go back in time and fight dinosaurs. Dinosaurs would probably be scared of tigers. That is, if they knew about them.'

'I like being called Stephen.'

'That doesn't matter! We'll change our names. We'll need disguises for when we go to space.'

I looked at him then. We stood next to the spaceship together, our feet trapped in cold mud. Stephen wiggled his hand out of mine. He ran his fingers along the edge of the spaceship. The paint crusted off and left orange flakes in his palm.

'No thanks,' he said, 'I think I want to sit with Charlotte.'

'Oh,' I said. I held out a char sui bao, but he had already gone.

I had to sit opposite Stephen in maths. He was talking to his *new best friend* about cats and butterfly hairclips. Luckily, the tears on my cheeks had dried into coarse patches.

'Now that we've spent ages together, I think we should get married,' said Charlotte. She winked vaguely at Stephen.

'What?' he said.

'It's never too early to start thinking about it,' she said. 'Daddy says I'm so pretty; I'll definitely get married.'

'Do you even want to get married?'

'Everybody wants to get married!' Charlotte flipped her hair. 'Even *Mei*!'

I stared at her. Stephen stared at the trapezoid on his worksheet.

'I don't want to get married,' said Stephen.

'I bet Mei wants to be your girlfriend.'

Charlotte smiled at me. I wanted to throw up on her.

'Shut up,' I said, 'Shut up, shut up, shut up!'

I stood up and grabbed a rubber. I threw it right into Charlotte's stupid face. We stood there for a bit. Then, she started bawling.

'Oh, dear. Dear!' Mrs. Key ran straight towards us. 'What's the matter, sweetie?'

'Mei is a *freak*!'

'Don't say that, honey. I know she's *different*, but that doesn't mean she's a freak.'

'She is a *monster*! She thinks that just because she's ugly she can be mean to anyone she wants,' she said, cloyingly. 'She hit me! I *hate* her!'

Mrs. Key turned to me.

'*Mei!*' she shrieked, 'How dare you treat another student like that!'

My face was hot. I wanted to crawl into a hole and scream. I picked up the pencil pot and threw it across the table. Then, I ran out of the classroom. In the distance, I could hear Mrs. Key.

'Why can't you be good, like Stephen? He has no problem fitting in!' she said, but I didn't care. I ran until the air felt rusty. Then, I imagined the bits in my lungs were stardust, and if I tried hard enough, I could grow a propeller and fly away. I sat in Stephen's spaceship, howling.

I thought about Mum, and her story about the jade rabbit in the moon:

'There was a god,' she said. 'The god went to the humans to ask them for food. The humans laughed at him, so the god asked the animals for something to eat. The animals all gave him food,' she said. 'The rabbit cooked herself so the god could eat. The god was pleased. As a reward, he turned her into the moon.

But the jade's lying beneath the flames now. She's not really a rabbit anymore.'

It was Stephen who found me. I don't think anyone else bothered to look.

'Do you want me to braid your hair?' he asked.

'I don't want to be your girlfriend,' I said.

'I know,' he said, and held his own long, black hair. 'Take two strands and fold them in.'

I stared. He smiled. 'Look, like this. It's like punching a dinosaur!'

I sat still. I didn't really know what else to do.

'I'm sorry,' I said, after a while. 'I think Stephen is a nice name.'

'Thank you,' he said. 'I think so, too.'

I held up two Char Siu Bao and he took one. I finished mine first, so I watched him eat his. We sat in the spaceship together, in silence.

We were two astronauts watching the paint peel.

# One Wednesday in June

## Eleanor Gray

# One Wednesday in June

## AIKO

The morning dew chills Aiko's knees as she kneels next to her flower bed, clawing the earth back into the gaping hole she's left in the garden. Soil packs itself beneath her nails – she'd even painted them for last night's dinner party, and the wives had loved them – but she's forgotten her gloves. She doesn't think about them now; her mind is preoccupied with checklists. Sleepless nights spent needling concealed pockets into clothing for personal documents, and packing a single bag with enough food, medicine and money to tide them over but not look suspicious if someone were to search her. She is lucky they're travelling in the summer – Makito is all too eager to talk about what frostbite can do to you. Check, check, check.

Next to her, the azaleas relax against a laundry basket of bones wrapped in muddy sheets. Any other year, Aiko would be overjoyed at her spring flowers blooming into the warmth of June. How will they fare without the bodies that were buried beneath them for so long? Or without her to pray for their souls? May the gods forgive her.

Aiko had always wanted a baby girl to adorn in shades of Heather and Lilac – to love, even in the cruellest month. Instead, she has her flower bed, and she doesn't mind so much because Makito made it when he was all she needed – beauty borne of horror, desperation, and hope. She still has her shades of Lilac, only now Aiko is glad she and her husband couldn't conceive their mixing; memory and desire.

*Our Rose by any other name would kill us, my dear.*

She adjusts the plants to the finest detail – those dinner party wives sure love to look at the flowers, and there couldn't be any risks taken – and rolls a white lily bulb around in her palm. But it's a Wednesday, and no one expects to die on a Wednesday, so she places it into the flower bed. Maybe it's a mother's intuition.

Aiko rises to her feet, places her trowel into a nearby bucket, and drags the laundry basket into the house. It's heavier than she thought it would be, considering it's mostly bones. And as she lugs it past the go-bag next to the back door and up the stairs, a muffled rattling cries out with every step, every stride, every pace – every other word she can think of to distract from the god-forsaken rattling.

She gets to the bedroom and places the quilt on the floor, right next to the jerry can. The dinner party wives had loved their room – couldn't stop snooping around for something scandalous to gossip about at their Friday morning tea clubs she is rarely invited to. And even if she is, what does it matter? The wives of Japanese monsters twittering about how great Oolong is (even though it's not) rather than their husband's jobs because it's easier to pretend they don't know (even though they do).

The female bones are encased in the first sheet (Makito said it was essential to keep them separate from the male set), each likely from a different host, equalling a set of remains similar to Aiko's height. She reaches for the skull, wiping away the excess dirt and loose hair, and finds herself staring at something she knows isn't her but still can't separate herself from.

This was a girl – multiple girls, but to her, just one. She was married to a man she no longer recognised but clung to the memory of the kindness that had built her a flower bed, the one that held her through each month of disappointed tears. She painted her nails to make the tea group think she was worthy of their mediocre drinks and malicious gossip. And she read poetry to forget how horribly, awfully, destructively afraid she was.

Aiko turns the skull, absorbing every dent and cavity as if it were her own. When Makito had brought this head home all those months ago, she'd almost been sick when he said they looked similar. "You'll have to trust me", he'd said, "you both have the same bone structure." She always wondered what was going through his head when he severed hers – the woman that looked like Aiko.

*It doesn't matter what he thought.* And in almost the same breath, but a different one nonetheless, *What a lie.*

Aiko places the skull on her pillow, angling it towards the centre of the bed. Next come the collar bones and ribs, the arms, the vertebrae. She turns each bone over, getting to know the notches and grooves, but she already knows all the parts – she has spent weeks studying Makito's books on skeletal anatomy and being quizzed by her husband. Maybe that's what passes for fun between them now.

Then, she sorts out her not-body in a position that feels right to both of them and fits the bones of 'Makito' (minus the head he is bringing home tonight) together like a macabre jigsaw puzzle before realising that this is how they sleep; facing one another, inches apart, but on separate shores of the Sea of Japan. She wishes he would love her from afar, where he can't touch her, and she can pretend he's the man she fell in love with, even after all this.

*Even on a Wednesday.*

She lifts the quilt and tucks in the bones with that motherly love before circling the bed to check her work. And she's not crying – she's not! – but saline pools form quietly along her socket line, and she wants to wipe them away, but she can't because she's dead. Yet the dead don't cry, and there's no use pretending it isn't happening. So she wraps her arms around herself to feel the heat of a life, asking herself how Makito could have done this to them. Not the one, not even the two, but the dozens of women with a severed leg or torso, and thought of his wife who only ever wanted to like Oolong tea and have a daughter.

But it's okay. No one has ever died on a Wednesday.

## SHÁN MIN

Shán Min glances behind him for a second, and another body has appeared; this one of a young half-woman (it's hard to tell with all the missing parts), ribs splaying open like a frog in an American biology class. One of their US donors had recently visited the facility and, in a liminal moment of small talk, had spoken to him about his daughter's science lessons. And a word the American had used to describe these frogs – one of the few words Shán Min knows fluently – was "red". This woman is indeed, perhaps by the very definition of the word, red.

Like the other Untouchables, Shán Min is a Chinese man enslaved on his own land, cleaning up the doctor's messes after a long day of play or ensuring stray corpses end up in the killing fields. Sometimes this means collecting up the prisoners that have been cast out of windows once playtime is over. Shán Min, however, is arguably the luckiest Untouchable here.

He had been passing by Shirō's office to be infected with cholera when the big boss was told about the information leak. The screaming was feral and petrified, and the guard escorting Shán Min stopped to check he was okay. After having his tantrum and hurling a few objects at those in the room, his eyes settled on the Untouchable like a lion spotting a gazelle. "You'll do," Shirō told him, spittle covering his chin. "Someone sent a letter to America about what we're doing here. I need you to find out who sent it." And Shán Min needed to stay alive, so he said yes.

Maybe he was chosen for his size – *mama said sunlight favours the farmers* – or his fluent understanding of Japanese, or maybe they just needed an informant, and he was walking by at the right moment. Or maybe it doesn't matter, because he made the mistake of looking over his shoulder once, only to find that he was red too, not by the very definition of the word, but perhaps some abstract form of it.

Shán Min turns back to the half-woman and drags her into the shallowest of graves, tossing what little soil there is into her body – he tries to fill the bodies before covering them, but today there's not even enough loose earth to do that.

"How are they today?" someone asks him, meaning the dead, and Shán Min again makes the mistake of looking over his shoulder.

Makito is dressed in full-body rubber gear, mask and all, and is upset about it (it's hiding his fancy suit).

"Good afternoon, sir," Shán Min says with a bow, "the dead are most forgiving today. I hope they treat you in similar esteem."

Makito glances at the Untouchable and nods (he had not bothered to listen to the response) before trudging into the killing fields – not so far back that he might hit the really, *really* dead people, but just far enough where they are dead enough not to spill his secrets. From the facility, Makito looks like any other employee.

At first, Shán Min saw nothing unusual; it wasn't out of the question for doctors to retrieve parts for further examinations, but over time, he noticed Makito behaved differently. He ventured much further into the killing field than his colleagues, and he was browsing for something very specific each time. The body parts Makito took never returned to the killing fields either – they weren't even chucked through a window – and he never took the same piece twice. Shán Min always suspected him of being some perverted Frankenstein.

But here's the odd thing: Makito isn't taking just female pieces anymore – he hasn't for some time.

Shán Min, more perplexed than disgusted, watches the surgeon remove a bone saw from the leather Gladstone bag that never leaves his side and begins hacking at the neck of a fresh (words become loose in a place like this) body – one that Shán Min remembers burying. A young man, big, probably with a proud mother who says he grows because the sunlight favours him.

And that's another odd thing: Makito had insisted on this young man becoming an Untouchable – the doctors couldn't go near him until his death sentence. And the other surgeons had said, while Shán Min didn't see it himself, that the Untouchable had a passing resemblance to Makito – even made jokes about accidentally killing the surgeon instead.

And then, Shán Min considers the doctor's job; after the Americans visited, Makito announced the next day a fantastic idea, which switched his department and won himself into the director's favours: plague-infested flea bombs.

Makito is walking back towards the facility, his rubber boots smattered with what looks like mud but isn't, and a bag far heavier than the one he walked out with. What possible use could the doctor have for the head of a man that looks like him? Or enough body parts to make himself a family?

Makito passes Shán Min on his way back inside, who (with a bow, of course) wishes the doctor a pleasant evening.

He is ignored once more.

## MAKITO

Through his office's window, the sun bleeds into the horizon, filtering through the pines and disappearing behind the killing fields. A single body fresh from vivisection (with almost all the right pieces sewn in virtually all the wrong places) relaxes, unaffected by Makito's recent removal of his head, but given a half burial more than he had at death.

He can't look down at his bag, rotting and with hair peeking out of the zipper, carrying the choking scent of purulence he hasn't smelt since working on the lethality of new weapons. Too fresh; he should have killed the kid earlier.

Life has lingered since then, hanging in suspense until the next time he hears the snapping of bones or holds skin innocent enough that a scalpel slips right in, and Makito's mind remains forever trapped in his previous occupation. He's motionless, choking on the scent of alcohol rags, hearing the slapping of wet flesh he notices everywhere these days. It has been 112 weeks since he and Aiko had slept together.

*All the sun needs to do today is fall.*

But today, even that seemed like a trial for the gods.

A gentle rapping on the door drags Makito back to his reality, although this isn't much better. "Enter," he says.

A meek-looking Untouchable enters the room, his clothing draped over his skeletal figure. There is a code carved into his forehead, the surrounding skin discoloured with infection and pus, the message reading what he has been infected with: "*pX01/pX02*".

*Anthrax.*

"Good evening, sir," the Untouchable says with a heavy Chinese accent.

"For you." Between his fingerless hands is a note, crumpled into a pattern that matches his two misshapen limbs, and passes Makito the message: "*Office 310*".

"Thank you," Makito says, and the Untouchable leaves, intelligent enough not to remain in striking distance.

Makito trails behind, scoping the hallways. He runs his fingers along the window's bars, reminding himself of the ones that wiggle in their foundations, as if he can escape through the caged windows – as if everyone that tried wasn't shot dead. Today though, he was keeping his hands busy.

He arrives at office 310 and waits for the director's Untouchable to give a gentle rapping on the door. "Enter," the director calls, and Makito opens the door, his head bowing as deeply as his bitten-back disgust would allow.

Shirō is a pitiful-looking man, but the medals adorning his walls aren't what keep people in their place; it's his hand-me-down hatred. His brainwashing turns dizzy-tongued and impressionable young soldiers into chest-stompers and rapists. If it weren't for his beautiful, sad, distant Aiko with her poetry and azalea bed to remind him that a different life still exists, he might have turned out the same way.

The office is full of fellow scientists staring at one another in either awe or fear; Makito cannot tell which.

"Makito!" Shirō celebrates, shaking Makito's shoulders like a child trying to reach the last coin in their coin bank. "There he is. My Shinigami." Makito freezes at the name. If his heart weren't beating so fast, he feared it might stop altogether.

*Grim reaper.*

Shirō sits back at his desk, gesturing to an empty seat in front of him, thoughtfully left available by the other employees. "So, we have results for *Cherry Blossom at Night*."

"Already?" Makito asks as his co-workers fidget in their seats. "Good or bad, sir?"

"Both." Shirō smiles with palpable evil. "As you know, the fleas were dropped at 22:19 two nights ago." It's not just palpable now – Makito can taste bile in the air. "Everyone is dead."

"Sir?"

"Everyone who became infected died in less than three days. Your chosen mix of infections rotted people from the inside out. Your idea was arguably *too* successful." He is laughing now.

*My idea.*

Makito doesn't hear much of anything after that. The air becomes viscous, moving with a fluidity that absorbs voices and cheering alike. Glasses clink together: the ritual celebratory intoxication of mass murder.

*It was my idea.*

"Makito, listen, we're having a get-together this weekend to celebrate, but until then, we will brainstorm a longer-lasting infection."

*It was my idea. But it doesn't matter; I had to. The months of planning and burying and studying – everything was for our survival. Please say Aiko had the courage to dig up those poor people and lay them out correctly. Please let us go, so she may one day look at me without fear and disgust in her eyes. Just a few more hours, please.*

And with a brief goodbye and a few feigned smiles, Makito leaves, trudging back to his office to gather his belongings on his last day. Whatever happens now, he knows this is his last day working at the unit. He doesn't even notice the Untouchable building up the courage to knock on the door of office 310 – the only one in the entire facility not given a death sentence. But he has no interest in talking with Makito anymore.

*Oh God, please let me go. I miss myself.*

## AIKO

Makito came home someone else today. He was not the man he had been the past few years, nor the person she fell in love with; he was someone else altogether. This was a cold man just trying to make it through the day: someone she'd needed through the nights spent opening seams and counting money while her husband slept.

Quietly and quickly.

Makito is upstairs, untucking the bodies and checking them for any inaccuracies in their layout, unable to find any, which – even though he would never admit it – is a pleasant surprise. He doesn't like to belittle or upset his wife ever – not when she failed at the thing she wanted most.

Quietly and quickly.

Downstairs, Aiko slips on her shoes. The go-bag is wrapped around her shoulders, and over it, a jacket weighed down with secret pockets. But tonight is the night, and layered over the usual contempt and fear, there is another emotion: hope. The same bittersweet feeling they faced every month – through it all, together, then and now.

Quietly and qui–

A knock on the door.

As Aiko freezes, her eyes round like that of a hunted rabbit, Makito becomes visible at the top of the stairs, mouth gaping as if he can't get enough air. He moves down the stairs with a fluidity she hasn't seen from him before, but she can imagine him moving the same way at work, like a snake hiding in a tree.

He appears hot and heavy at her side, breathless. "Was that the door?"

Then, another knock, louder this time. So she isn't hearing things (she knew that already, but if the mind can do anything at all, it's hope blindly) because now Makito is wide-eyed and vacant. Perhaps he's already dead. But no one knocks three times: not in the middle of the night.

*It's the neighbours, it has to be, asking about their lost cat. Or maybe one of the wives asking if we've seen her bracelet after the dinner party – the clasp probably broke, but it's gold with a daisy pattern. She knows I don't have it, but accusing me of theft would keep them entertained for at least a day.*

And finally, a third. Louder. More insistent.

The silence that comes with it is a heavy one.

But it's a Wednesday.

# Fool's Gold

## Ella Lounds

# Fool's Gold

Once upon a time, a farmer lived in a poor kingdom with his wife and their daughter. She was pretty enough, but her true value was in the cloth she wove. She often laboured for days at a time, and the cloth was the finest in all the nearby villages, which brought the family a small but sufficient income. With time, however, the girl came of marriageable age, and though her pleasant features drew many an eye, just as many were turned away by her unbrushed hair and preference for weaving over conversation. The farmer received a few offers for her hand, but none were good enough for his daughter—or, in truth, for his own ambition.

One day, when the local Baron was riding through the market, he saw some beautiful cloth on sale. He asked to meet the weaver, and the farmer led him to their home, talking all the while of his daughter's beauty and skill. When she greeted the baron, he was so taken by her humility—she could not look him in the eye!—that he proposed at once. The farmer was so thrilled he allowed his daughter a request: to speak to the Baron alone before the marriage was finalised.

The girl told the Baron that her father was using her to gain power and prestige, and that she would make a dreadful wife, for she was more interested in weaving than men. She showed him her loom, and spoke for the rest of the hour about the intricacies of manufacturing cloth. When her father returned, she gave the Baron a small but exquisite tapestry. He thanked her, but withdrew his offer of marriage, giving her a golden necklace in apology.

The farmer was furious, but his daughter promised that she'd been kind and polite and that the Baron seemed perfectly content to listen to her talk. The farmer was frustrated, and told her not to talk to the next suitor, but he did not mind, for it was only a Baron.

Some months later, an Earl visited the Baron. He saw the tapestry in the Baron's castle and inquired as to its origin. The Baron led the Earl to the farmer, who fell at his feet and sang the praises of his beautiful daughter. Upon meeting her, the Earl was so taken by her slender hands that he proposed at once. Her father was thrilled, and allowed his daughter to speak to the Earl alone, after reminding her of her promise.

The girl told the Earl nothing, but led him to her loom, where she wove for the entire hour in silence. When her father returned, she handed the Earl a small but beautiful tapestry. He thanked her, but withdrew his offer of marriage, giving her a diamond-studded ring in apology.

The farmer was furious, but his daughter swore that she'd kept her promise and not said a word. Next time, the farmer said, he would not let her speak to any suitor before their wedding night.

After a year passed with no further proposals, the farmer began to despair. Perhaps they should glorify her to the Prince, his wife suggested, and the Prince would introduce her to some Lord a long way from their village. And so the two set off, carrying their daughter's most beautiful tapestry yet as a gift for the Prince.

Once they arrived, the Prince greeted them kindly and listened to their tale. They told him of their daughter, the beautiful girl with lovely face and hair like the finest cotton thread. Their daughter, the finest seamstress in the world, who'd single-handedly crafted the tapestry they'd brought with them, and could weave cloth as soft as a cat's fur. Their daughter, so talented she could weave straw into gold, if only she had a loom that could withstand the strain.

Their daughter, whom every suitor rejected after just an hour alone in her presence.

The Prince listened to their story, which they gave earnestly despite the lies woven into the plea. He spoke with his advisors and drew up a contract: if she truly could weave straw into gold, he said, he would marry her, no matter what. The farmer and his wife were thrilled, and signed the contract without hesitation.

They returned to their village with the Prince, and invited him into their home. He spoke to the girl, and asked her to weave a scarf for his elderly grandmother, whose skin could only bear the softest of materials. The girl nodded and set to work, unspeaking. When she had finished, the Prince took the cloth and ran it between his hands. It was soft, softer than he had ever felt, and he smiled at her. She did not smile back, and still she did not speak.

The Prince invited her to his palace, and explained the contract he had signed. He would marry her within the week, he said, provided she pass three tasks. The first and second, she had managed already: her face was indeed lovely, and she had woven cloth soft as duckling down. The final test, he said, would bring their kingdom back to prosperity, and land her a seat at the Prince's right hand.

The final test, the Prince explained once they arrived at his palace, was to weave gold from straw. He led her to small room atop a tower, which held a sturdy loom, a tub of water, a rolling pin, several hackles, a distaff, a spinning wheel, and an enormous pile of straw.

The girl surveyed the room, considered crying, and picked up a single stalk of straw instead. She snapped it easily and peered inside; as she suspected, it had not been retted. She frowned, considering other crafts she could attempt, and began soaking a handful of straw in the tub of water. As she waited for the straw to soften into a flexible state, she examined the loom. It was a beautiful dandy loom, and while she preferred a manual treadle loom, she knew its dandy mechanism was exquisitely made.

As the moon rose, silvery light filled the room, and she settled herself in a corner and began folding the straw into doilies. After several hours, she heard the loom start moving, and looked up, meeting the eyes of a small man.

'Who are you?'

'That would be telling,' he said. 'Straw into gold?' She nodded.

'Marriage or death?'

'Hopefully not.'

'Need a little help, then?' She held up a doily from the pile beside her. 'I'm quite comfortable,' she said.

'That's not gold,' said the man.

'I know,' she said. 'It's not possible to make gold from straw. It's not even possible to make cloth from this straw, it's not been processed. There's no scotching knife here either, and frankly I hate spinning thread anyway. My father is terrible about metaphors, he just says the most outlandish things and never clarifies them at all. I'm certain this has all been a misunderstanding.'

The man blinked. 'Do you want me to spin this straw into gold?'

'The Prince only wants me to enrich the kingdom. You can if you wish, but I would rather go home.'

'And stay with the family who keeps trying to sell you off?'

The girl paused and considered this. 'I don't like change,' she said.

The man smiled, his mouth a gash across his face with too many teeth. "I don't think you have much choice."

'No,' she said. 'I suppose not. Very well: you spin two skeins of golden thread. One, I will weave into cloth, the other I will keep as thread. I will give him the cloth, and on my wedding day, you will return and take me away. I will use the gold to weave even more beautiful tapestries, and remain a spinster until the day I die.'

'This is most unusual,' the man said. 'And what do I get in return?'

'I can give you the ring from my finger,' said the girl, 'or the necklace from my neck.'

'I can spin straw into gold,' said the man, 'what need do I have for expensive trinkets?'

'I can give you company,' she said, 'someone to talk to, someone to weave the thread you spin.'

'I enjoy my own company.'

'Then what did you have in mind?'

'Your firstborn child.'

'I don't intend on having children. Besides, that's very exploitative.'

'It seems we are unable to reach an agreement,' the man said, and got to his feet. 'Farewell, Princess. I hope the Prince likes your doilies.'

'Wait,' she said. 'There's one more thing I have left to offer.'

He paused.

'Your name.'

'My name?'

'It's Rumpelstiltskin, is it not?'

'How did you know?'

The girl laughed, eyes devoid of pity. 'You think that none know of Rumpelstiltskin? Your name is shared in whispers from each princess to her subjects, from each mother to her daughter, and each girl to her friends. Every woman in this country knows of you.'

'You wicked girl!' he cried. 'You wretched child!'

'You can't leave until I say, can you? You are bound to my service, correct?'

He did not reply, but the girl continued.

'Spin me two skeins of gold. That is all I ask. In return, I will free you from my service.'

The man snarled and set to work, and when the prince returned that morning, he found the princess hard at work, spinning golden thread into gold cloth. He rejoiced, certain that his kingdom was saved from poverty, and the girl did not correct him.

On their wedding night, Rumpelstiltskin returned, spiriting the girl away just as the Prince arrived to their room. The Prince cried out for his guards, but it was too late: his Princess was gone, never to be seen again.

# Five Poems

## Naomi Parker

## Pretender

I always go back for more blood.
The look is not complete without the blood.
If the blood comes off, who am I then?
Sometimes you don't realise just how bad things are
Until you're sat on the kitchen floor at 2am
Trying to strangle yourself with your Halloween costume.

## Pentes

I won't see two vacant windows
Slow encroaching nature
Or bitter rind
That never makes it to the pan
I'll never know the town that keeps on changing
Those strange smiling faces
Or the street
Where Margaret's tearoom can be found
I won't look inside the freezer
Find no waiting heart
No bags of fruit
No plans.

## Marmalade

Instead
I see the colour green
Bright skies
And a small mug of warm tea against my palms.
Fragrant forest fruit infusions
And the sharp scent
 Of real oranges in the background.
I'll always see that vat of marmalade
Mismatched jars
And tiny labels
Written by your hand.

## Our Fridays

she's bathed in warmth
as she turns up at your door
her raft in chaos waters.
she wears her heeled boots
as if she could belong
storming the waitrose aisles
for jersey royal potatoes.

you chew your bottom lip
quietly displeased
at the ever-growing crowd
lingering like vultures.
how can she compare?
always hanging back

yet you give her this light
each Friday.

## when fish can't swim

must i give in
to these abstract intrusions?
the sharks speak loudest in my head.
*one missing fish does not disturb the sea.*

# Broken Mirror

## Beth Robertson

# Broken Mirror

Officer Sammy Ross had never paid much attention to her reflection, but something about today made her stare at it for a little longer than usual.

Through the window of the police car, she caught glimpses of her mirrored face as it flashed over the outside world. As she reached a hand up to scratch her head, her reflection mimicked every move with the same nervous energy as its living counterpart.

*Wellness checks are nothing to worry about*, Victor had told her on her first call, *they are always either a waste of time because the person is fine, or they are the run-of-the-mill breakdowns, people wound too tight by the daily stresses of life. Nothing more, nothing less.* Sammy had thought him heartless when he first said this, but now she knew better. Sure, he could've phrased his point with more tact, but he was right.

Even so, something about this call gave Sammy an odd feeling deep in her chest.

*A mother is concerned for her daughter's safety after receiving a flurry of texts about her daughter's "reflection being frozen." The daughter has no history of psychosis or other mental health issues other than anxiety. The daughter lives with her boyfriend in a small, terraced house. Both are in their early twenties and are university students.*

*Reflection being frozen.* What did that mean?

'Most likely a psychotic episode resulting in hallucinations,' came a voice from her right. Sammy glanced at the driver of the car, Victor Duran, and rolled her eyes in mock annoyance.

'At least let me ask the question first.'

Victor smirked, his version of a laugh.

'I saved you the trouble.'

Sammy returned to gazing out the window just in time to see the street of terraced houses come into view. Victor slowed the car down in front of one and stopped the engine.

'Here we are.'

The gate squeaked as Victor pushed it open, and together the two police officers passed through the small garden to the front door. The paint on both the house and door were faded, and the garden was ever so slightly overgrown.

Victor knocked, and the pair waited as the usual shuffling of people reacting to a door knock was heard, followed by silence. Sammy was about to suggest he knock again before the door creaked open and a tall, tanned man with dark hair and eyes peeked out. Upon recognising their uniforms, he opened the door further, and Sammy could see he was wearing pyjamas.

'Hello?' The word was less of a greeting and more of a question. *What the hell are the police doing here?*

'Good morning, sir,' Victor replied, 'My name is DI Victor Duran, and this is my partner, Sammy Ross. We are here to conduct a wellness check on Miss Robin Smith, is she in?'

The man pulled the door open fully.

'Who called for a wellness check?' His voice had a clear American accent, though Sammy couldn't pinpoint which state it was from.

'Her mother,' Victor replied. 'Is Robin inside?'

The man paused; his eyes were blank.

'So, she...' A moment later they regained life, and he leant on the doorframe in resignation. 'Right, sure.'

He stepped aside and allowed the pair to enter. Sammy attempted a reassuring smile as she passed; he didn't look much older than her.

'She's in the bedroom,' the man said, pointing up the stairs to their left, 'But I think I should go first. I didn't... we weren't expecting this.'

Without waiting for an answer, the man passed the officers and started up the stairs. Sammy looked to Victor for direction.

'Californian,' he said with a small smile. Sammy sighed.

The stairs creaked underfoot, and the floorboards felt uneven. At the top was a small landing with multiple doors; the man pushed one open and poked his head around it. A few seconds of muttered conversation followed, in which Sammy only caught the word 'darling' being repeated. Quite the old-timey word for a couple of university students to use.

Finally, the man let them enter what turned out to be a small bedroom.

On the bed across from them sat a young woman, also wearing pyjamas. Her eyes were wide, and she looked between the two officers in silence. The man lowered himself onto the bed next to her, the bed sagging and creaking as he did. Sammy gave the woman a small wave as she navigated around a pile of clothes on the floor.

'Hi. It's Robin, right?' she asked. The woman nodded with no change in expression. Sammy faltered. 'It's alright... we're here to help.'

'Who called you?' Robin asked. Both officers had to lean forward to hear her.

'Your mother,' Victor replied. 'She is very worried about you.'

'I was just telling her the truth. Jake... Jake doesn't see it. I thought maybe...'

The man, Jake, put an arm around her and pulled her close, looking up at the officers as he did so.

'Robin woke me up this morning saying the bathroom mirror was broken,' he said, 'I thought she meant it had smashed or something, so I went to look at it, but it's fine. She keeps saying that her reflection has... stopped? Frozen? I don't know—'

'It has!' Robin interjected, staring straight at Sammy, 'It just... stares at me. Not doing anything. No matter how I move or what I do, it just... doesn't mimic me like a reflection should. It's messing with me; I know it is!' Robin put her head in her hands as Jake rubbed her back. 'He doesn't believe me...'

Sammy and Jake met eyes. She knew well the expression on Jake's face—the confusion, worry and shock that came with a call such as this.

'I don't know what's happening,' he said, 'The mirror is fine, I don't understand...'

Victor stepped forward.

'Would you mind if I looked at your phone, Robin? I would like to see the messages you sent to your mother.'

Jake reached behind him, unlocked the phone, then passed it to Victor, who scrolled through it for a few moments. All eyes remained on him, bar Robin who was trying to pull herself together. Eventually, the two women met eyes again.

'You have a look,' Robin said, her voice gaining a surprising amount of confidence.

Sammy blinked. 'I'm sorry?'

'The mirror. Have a look at it! Maybe you'll see.'

Sammy looked to Victor as Jake pleaded with Robin to 'not do this again'. Victor was still absorbed in the text messages. *Maybe it would make her feel more at ease...*

'Alright, let's see.'

Robin scrambled to her feet, relief in her eyes. Jake was stopped from following by a smile from Sammy. *She'll be okay.*

The two women wove through the scattered clothes until they reached the bathroom door, then paused. Robin placed a shaking hand on the handle.

'It's alright,' Sammy said, placing her hand on top of Robin's. Together they pushed the door open.

The bathroom was in the same state of disarray as the rest of the house.

Behind the bath, Sammy spotted a small mirror above the sink, cracked but whole. She approached it with an unusual amount of hesitance.

'What do you see?' Robin asked.

Sammy stared at her reflection. She ran a hand through her hair and mirror-Sammy followed suit, raising its left hand as Sammy raised her right and pushing it through her short mop of hair. She felt a confusing sense of relief upon seeing this. For the briefest of moments, she had believed her reflection wouldn't move. How silly a thought that was.

'My reflection... seems fine,' she replied, choosing her words carefully. But not carefully enough, it seemed, for Robin shoved her aside and stared at the mirror herself, then waved her arm frantically side to side. Mirror-Robin followed her every move.

'No... no, no, no...' she muttered. Sammy watched her chest rise and fall more rapidly, 'You can't do this again, no...'

Sammy held her hands up, meeting Robin's stare in the mirror as she spoke.

'Hey, it's alright—'

'It's *not* alright!' Robin cried, leaning on the sink and staring further into the mirror 'Why are you doing this? *Why?* What do you want from me?' She began to sob, her body heaving with distress. The two Robins on either side of the mirror stared at each other, the same pleading look in their eyes.

'Robin—'

Before Sammy could stop her, Robin screamed—a shrill, guttural sound—and punched the mirror, smashing it. Glass clattered on the sink as Sammy grabbed Robin's arm, pulling her away. Blood splashed on the white ceramic.

Everything froze.

Sammy stumbled backwards, and suddenly there was a bed behind her, and Jake and Victor were talking. She looked across at Robin but was met with Victor, and they were in the kitchen. He was saying something to her that she couldn't hear, and then there were new voices and flashes of blue, and Sammy wanted to sit down. If she sat down, maybe time would stop. She put a hand out to pull up a chair but was met with concrete. *How did concrete get into a kitchen—?*

A *slam* brought Sammy's thoughts screeching to a halt, and she was sat on the kerb outside Robin and Jake's house. An ambulance stood waiting in the middle of the road, and she watched two paramedics hop into the front of it.

'It is sad, really.'

Sammy jumped at Victor's sudden voice behind her. 'Who? What?' *What on Earth is going on?*

'Those two. They have been through a lot.'

*The paramedics? No, wait...*

'Jake and Robin, you mean?'

'Yeah. Financial difficulties, relationship issues, impending deadlines... your typical breakdown recipe.'

Sammy took this in for a moment, then shook her head.

'It's a shame,' she replied. Victor's footsteps echoed on the pavement behind her.

'It is life. What can you do?'

Sammy leant backwards, jumping when her back met the soft leather of a car seat. The ambulance pulled away in front of them, and the car rumbled as the engine sprang to life.

*Wellness checks are nothing to worry about.*

As they began their drive to the hospital, Sammy glanced out the passenger side window once more, catching a glimpse of her reflection again under the movement of the outside world.

She brought up a hand to fix her hair.

Her reflection did not follow.

# Three Poems

## Maya Shell

# *a dream in which i own a swimming pool*

i fill it with eight hundred Rennies
bought in bulk from the pound shop
dissolving them slowly

i dip my elbow in as a test
and slip into clouds of sediment
the colour of doves and loaves
or mildly anaesthetised teeth

i swim
mouth open
letting curled fingers cradle my face
hoping to soothe the sour thing that lurks
amongst the mists of talc in the locker room

it rolls through old women's lungs
like a goat's marbled eye off my palm
mapping the edges
and lying in wait

# *and so we kept moving forward*

up and over sand banks
where the hot mud sucked in cheeks
bracing them for the sharpness of crisps
and things heard from her sister's magazine

spitting darkness like peach pits
she cannot run more than a hundred meters
without a tapestry pulling tight on her lungs
dread building with a sticklebricked patience
silvered legs shining
and stained with tomatoes

# *dad lets me go to the Egypt exhibit by myself*

i don't care for the pots and dead cats; they are old news
broken things put back together
no— i am here for one thing only
the king is dead and we have come to see

with a decidedly flat nose
my girlbreath pushes white against glass
tongue running over sore gummed gaps
where ancient history has cut my mouth

# Three Poems

## Leah Sigsworth

# *Chrysanthemums and sunset pictures*

Metamorphosis of my anxiety,
whispers I am simply carbon and bad timing.
In moments, it is a ladybird in a tiger's grasp,
then, the tiger itself.
On those days I lay still until the predator passes.
Playing dead.
Dad suggests I buy myself some flowers,
in flowers I see remnants of her pyre in bloom.
The flesh of her crematorium.
Memory lulls me with eyes un-shut,
I sing her favourite songs with my eyes closed.
I am standing beside her coffin.
It is the moment I learn every person I ever love will come to die.

Anxiety is now the cousin from out of town that visited at her funeral,
he told me my eulogy "missed out some things".
Handed me a hug overflowing with panic attacks,
he's resided next door ever since.
I hear him in the walls in the night and he breathes sweat onto my
forehead.
He sets the table with a vacant chair.

The silent conversations in the hallway are your wake,
one where we all grow those same tiger claws and never mutter "I love you."
Mum's lips sealed so tightly like adhesive on stained glass,
one my sister throws drinks at and shouts "If there was a god why the fuck
did you die."
Dad murmurs "Instead of dying a jellyfish simply ceases to move."

# *I just wish you'd been honest.*

I watched Dad take down your bird box during the house clearance.
I stayed in the kitchen watching out the window,
air smelt like nail polish and burnt toast.
All I can picture is the field mice burrowing in your shoulders.

I still read your texts.

When the rain is tender I imagine it is your kiss,
on my cheek.
Sprouting grass from your eye sockets.
I rummaged through the cupboard looking for green tea,
no one told me there would still be soup in the back of your pantry.
It spills through the holes in your hollow bones.
It was out of date as it'd been there for years,
long expired.
Indecisiveness was enough to keep it stagnant. Never eaten.

You told me you weren't going anywhere. You lied.

I tried to keep some of your things, but it's difficult to store so much that
people are,
afraid
to use.
Your coffee cup was still stained,
insignificant and everywhere.

You told me you would see me soon. You lied.
Your coaster was thrown.

## *I only feel pretty when I am hungry*

The year of vodka shots for breakfast and laxatives for dessert.
Zero-calorie Monsters at lunchtime and rice cakes dipped in cups of tea
with no milk.
I skipped dinner.
Diets I found on Instagram,
half a passion fruit once every 48 hours, smoking, an apple (but only if I
fainted in the shower),
the military diet, and juices disguised as meals.
We toasted to finishing first year and he complimented my "new legs."
Why would I ever want to stop being hungry,
when not eating became the most interesting thing about me.
Eating in front of a mirror whilst we Facetimed and he told me,
"I am so turned on by you, you look so good."

My favourite jumper was falling apart and mum tried fixing it over Easter,
thought placing it in the tumble dryer,
low heat when I visited home,
would prevent further damage.
She didn't realise I had gone down 3 dress sizes in 4 weeks.
Or perhaps she did.

I tried donating blood,
snapping elastic bands around my wrist when I craved anything that wasn't
ice.
I remember the girls from school told me no man would ever "love me if I
was a fat bitch,"
It was my birthday, I tried flushing my cake down the toilet.
They were right.
They told me "Nothing tastes as good as skinny feels."

What if I still don't feel much at all?
Anything except being cold in a warm room,
or the desperation to Google how many calories are in the glue of an
envelope.
Or a pea size squeeze of toothpaste.

A salad with no dressing.
I accidentally spill too much salt into my pasta and I tell mum I cannot eat it.
I see a banana and I see 58 press-ups and a handful of squats.
I watch Supersize Vs Superskinny on repeat, crying into an empty mug of hot chocolate,
hiding Saxenda I bought from eBay under my bed.
He still carries my underwear photos in his wallet,
and tells me I am a success story.

# Monopoly-Night Mayhem

---

## Kalon Douglas Torr

# Monopoly-Night Mayhem

Lightning danced amongst the clouds and, within their veins, a mass without form fell from the sky. The thunder roared; we chuckled our fright away.

'I hope the owls are okay,' Jess said.

'They'll be fine, they're tough,' I replied.

I tilted my eyebrows towards Jess, the Monopoly board, and then back at Jess.

'Dad, everyone needs to be here.'

'Well, we could steal from his pile... he is kind of beating us both.'

'Don't lump me in with you, I'm doing just fine.'

Our bickering was interrupted by Mark walking back into the room with a wide grin across his face.

'Anyone steal from my pile?'

Jess pointed at me, stretching her arm out so far that it crossed the entire board.

'You know what I told you about lies; she's framing me, that's what this is,' I said, darting my head between Jess and Mark.

'I didn't steal from your pile,' I responded.

Mark looked me up and down. He didn't buy it.

'Okay, well I would have, and I would've gotten away with it wasn't for that meddling kid.'

The two looked at me with deadpan faces, wishing to be anywhere but here. I smiled back, matching Mark's earlier grin.

Without warning the power cut out, leaving us in darkness. Lighting flashed and we were able to see each other's faces for a moment. Standing up, I fumbled for my phone and turned the flashlight on. A booming screech echoed through the house, followed by the faint crunching of gristle and bone.

'What's going on?' Jess said, now clinging onto my leg.

'I don't know.'

'We're leaving,' Mark commanded.

'Yeah,' I replied, my gaze now following the footsteps on the roof.

In a coordinated panic we rushed towards the garage and then to the car. Mark smacked the button by the entrance and let it rattle open. He made his way back towards the driver's seat and started the engine up. A cloud of black fumes burst from the exhaust as it rattled into life. The headlights flicked on, and we all froze in a dumbfounded terror. A towering imitation of an owl blocked the exit. The body was made up of a bubbling sludge, coloured like oil. The beak, malformed and grotesque, let out a putrid stench that encased the car in an aroma of death. As it roared and shook our spines, Jess buried her head into my side.

Mark put the car in first and slammed down on the accelerator. The engine roared as the car launched into the beast. It reacted in an instant and flung itself upwards. It held in the air before diving and plunging its talons into the car's hood. Mark pressed harder on the accelerator, now locked in an unwinnable tug of war by his own stubbornness.

'Jess, get out!' I cried.

I opened the door and we both crashed onto the floor. Oblivious, Mark raged against the steering wheel. The beast dug its talons deeper into the hood and lifted the car into the sky. Mark's screaming faded as the beast flew higher and higher into the clouds. For an inescapable moment, the only sound was Jess' quiet sobbing, until the car crashed onto the ground. A thin layer of blood trickled out of the caved-in roof and onto our flower bed. The beast landed atop the car, causing blood to spurt out. It glared at us with eyes void of soul, of empathy, or love. I was sure, then, weren't food to it, just toys. Holding in vomit and tears, I grabbed Jess and bolted back into the house.

We steadied and caught our breath, the adrenaline still pulsating through us both. Jess drifted away from me, I shivered, feeling my tear-soaked top meet the cold air.

'It's gonna be okay; we're gonna be okay.'

Giving her a faint smile, I wiped the tears from her face and clutched her hand. Outside, the metal of the car grated against itself as it was contorted. The sound of flesh and bone being devoured followed soon after. I moved us both away from the door and the faint tapping of feet followed us from the garage floor. They carried a stench of raw sewage and petrol, churning my stomach. The door handle began to rattle and then, with a steadier hand, it was pushed downwards. The door waved open.

'Into the kitchen,' I said, with a tremble in my speech.

Jess stood motionless.

'Now, Jess!'

As Jess darted away, a humanoid figure entered, leaking black sludge and bile onto the carpet. What was left of the wings slumped onto the floor and writhed as if conscious. It resembled Mark in a way, though I tried not to dwell on that as I darted into the kitchen like a scared deer unbound from a headlight's spell. I slammed the door behind me and, after propping a chair against it, my hands dove onto a knife rack and drew the longest one I could. I turned to see Jess curled up into a tight ball under a table quivering; a scared child lost in their own mind.

'What happened to Dad?' She asked.

'We've gotta go,' I responded, unable to face the fact myself.

She paused for a moment, then nodded. Tears falling from her eyes I took her in my arms and squeezed her tight, allowing the tears to fall from mine.

'We're going to be okay.'

The beast howled and barged into the door. Pleading that time had passed slower, I let go and pulled her from under the table.

'I need you to go into town, okay. Do you remember the way?' I said, standing her up.

'What?'

'You gotta get help.'

'What about you?'

'I'm staying.'

'You can't! I can't...'

The beast bashed the door again, rattling the hinges.

'I have to, okay? I have to.'

Enraged, she pulled away from me.

'I'm not leaving you!'

The beast wailed against the door, shaking the house. The hinges now hung by a thread and the chair was ready to snap in two.

'You've got to be brave!'

Silent, she sagged, accepting that I wouldn't back down. I picked her up and passed her through the window.

'You got this,' I said.

She nodded and ran into the night.

I spun around as the chair shattered and door flew open, hurling splinters towards me. The beast stepped forward and into the kitchen, its presence wriggling across my skin. Wearing its mangled face, it glared at me, as if taunting, wanting me to lunge for it so it could consume me. I reached for an empty glass on the side and flung it at the imitation. It caught it and shattered the glass within its grasp. I went through the door beside me and entered the living room. Before I could gather myself, the beast burst through the door. In a wild panic, I flung round and severed its arm with my knife. The arm squirmed as it evaporated away. The beast screamed and the sludge ran from its face like tears. I moved away, flailing the knife in its direction. It continued towards me. In its eyes now was not emptiness, but rage, a fierce malice directed at me and me alone. The beast reached out for the knife and, pushing me back, I slipped on the Monopoly board. My bearings scattered as I fell to the floor. The beast gripped my ankle, and I howled in pain as my bones splintered. I slashed into its wrist and splattered the sludge over the floor. The beast wailed and let go. My foot fell to the floor in a sad, agonizing thump.

Trying to crawl away, my hands pushed against the Monopoly board and its pieces, sending them flying but keeping me trapped in place. The beast stopped and, as if in thought, watched me. Was it mocking me? Letting my embarrassment fuel my torment. I waited for it to finish me. Instead, a gargle came from its throat, a hoarse grating to my ears.

'I'm not,' it mumbled, 'I'm not going to leave you.'

I froze. It was Mark's voice, raspy and filtered, but true.

'You're going to be okay,' he said.

He took a step forward, and another, and another. Dropping the knife, I let him. Now he stood over me and the strength ran from my body like water down a stream. What was once an imitation now seemed infallible; a flawless reflection of what was. Gentle now, he placed his palm on my face. It spread across my head, sinking into my skin and mouth. The sludge engulfed my body, running through my veins and resting within my lungs. As my heart pumped it around me, my insides boiled, my liver turned to mush and my intestines to jelly. Rotting away, it tickled.

# Five Poems

## Meg Whitelock

## *Untitled*

You could
Measure your milestones
In the distance between the moles on my left cheek
Or from the corner of my lip to its bow
Use your index and trace the route
And realise it is easy

I say you may use me as a guide
So if my eye colour would help you,
Take it

Consider though
You would have my face be so different
If you were to stray
Even a little
If you would misremember the point of my nose slope
You would not recognise me from your accidents

## Injure me and my skin

A nerve
Runs thick
And fast through my left elbow
To the tip of my middle finger
Unlike my loathing
Like rotation is unchangeable
Malleable/ I will indulge you

Praise
Of my curves
Of my efficient maturity
Feeds me like nothing else will

## Untitled

A child of four discovers a corpse
Yet instead
Envy

Or       say       instead of pain
They resent
Their mother

## Circa 2000

It took you
And you hadn't expected harsh summer

For skin

I look forward
On nights
To be put to work

That rare thing
Warms

And gives to you
Something lasting
From its own perfumery

## They do not

Friends say your sweet smell diseases my gums but
My collarbone is your design

I say

My memory is a side-effect of something I think you did to me

      Too much/ and too much
wine/ almost enough to sleep like I
used to

So splintered bed frames stay restless      here
And they do not stop for my mother

# Our Gifts Are Curses in Shiny Wrapping

## Laura Wilson-Deakin

# Our Gifts Are Curses in Shiny Wrapping

'Poor Helen. She won't escape a witchcraft charge,' I said, hopping over a dislodged cobble in the road. 'Better her than us, I suppose.'

'Hopefully they're too focused on finding the fakes to bother us,' Maisie said.

We spoke freely in the centre of the city, other conversations and quarrels drowning out our secrets. I had always loved that about Edinburgh—that you could walk down a street full of people and be totally invisible. It certainly pays to be able to hide when the entire country would have you burnt at the stake if they knew what you were, how powerful you were. After twenty-three years running from the authorities and our neighbours alike, I had learned how to live each day like it could be the last one I had with magic flowing through me.

'Can we stop at The Fudge House? You can't get fudge like they make it anywhere else in Edinburgh, maybe even the world,' I said, taking two steps for every one of Maisie's just to keep up with her. She had always been much taller than me even though she was three years younger, but I liked to think I made up for it in personality.

She stopped in the middle of the street to the annoyance of the busy shoppers around us. 'We're supposed to be on the ward in half an hour!' Maisie carried on walking without waiting to see if I was following. I knew she loved me really, just had a funny way of showing it. She turned the corner at the end of the road that opened onto the Royal Mile. Here there were even more people littering the streets—ladies with much less to do with their day than us sat at tables outside drinking tea and gossiping.

'Do you know if Nancy had hers yet? I couldn't bear to leave her,' I asked as the castle came into view.

'Not yet. The first one is always the worst,' she said.

'Is it always worth it? I mean, some wee bairns seem like they set out to give their mam hell from birth.' I hadn't become a midwife because I loved the little bundles of sick. It was where I could make the most difference in the world without having my magic uncovered. My power could help the women through the pain that had been unfairly forced upon them.

'I couldn't say, *m'eudail*. I think the entire experience is different when you go through it yourself,' she said, not looking me in the eye anymore. Her curse wasn't as touchy a subject as it had once been, but I knew it still hurt to talk about. She often brushed it off, saying that there are some things even a powerful witch like me can't fix. I never forgot that.

'I suppose so.' Silence brewed between us as we continued walking towards the castle. It wasn't an uncomfortable silence—we were too close for that. It was more of a solemness we both understood.

The castle could be seen from far down the Royal Mile. It was almost as old as my family and I often felt their energies in every step I took around the area, heard their whispers on the back of children's chatter. It was a comfort for them to be there, especially since I was so young when my parents died. They were a warm breath against my cheek, a shot of adrenaline when I needed it the most. I always sensed that Mam was proud of me since I filled her shoes at the hospital—she loved midwifery like she did my father and I. It became one of my greatest loves too.

After we passed the castle, still in our solemn silence, it began to rain. The clouds changed from sterile white to ash grey in minutes.

'Maisie, we're going to be soaked!' I pulled my coat around myself to protect my uniform. The bottom of my pinafore had already been splashed with murky puddle water and I swore I could hear sloshing in my shoes.

'We'll just have to walk a wee bit quicker then, won't we?' she said with a smile. She took a few more steps before jumping in a puddle that had formed in a dip in the road. Dirty water splashed up the side of my coat but it was well worth it to see her grin like a small child. It was only later, as we passed the Waldorf Astoria, that I realised I hadn't been splashed with just water.

There was blood in that puddle too.

Young witches were taught that blood in water was a sign of trouble, but I failed to register it before it was too late.

~

Walking into the maternity ward was the same whether I was taking a day or night shift—the air stung with magic and set my fingertips twitching, eager to work. The other midwives and I shared a lot in common, not only because we were all hiding from persecution but because we were all healers. We could take the pain from other women, diminish its potency and experience it ourselves. It was one of the most privileged positions within the coven. But it required a support network such as ours to cope with the strong emotional demand of that privilege.

Helen Murray's arrest gnawed at me for most of the day, but I didn't discuss it with any of the other girls on the ward. I felt foolish for worrying so much. The police hadn't arrested me, or any other practising witch. However, she had only been *pretending* to possess the gift that I cherish and they'd made a spectacle of arresting her. What would they have done with one of us? Would they have skipped prison and put us straight onto the stake? I spilled boiling water all over the kitchen worktop thinking about it on my break.

I had finished mopping the quietest section of the ward when the air shifted. It wasn't the shift I felt when a woman arrived on the ward—there was usually just a hint of panic that diffused into the air. This time there was a tidal wave of anxiety and desperation from the other witches, drowning the entire hospital in terror. The power within me shook my insides. I gripped the mop so hard a splinter broke my skin, but the sensation was far away, unable to break through the wall of dread in my mind.

Maisie appeared at the door, eyes wide and searching. The look she sent my way had my magic growing wild—I felt it escaping my control but there was nothing I could do to stop it.

'Iona, you have to go!'

'What do you mean?' I asked, my voice shaking.

'One of the patients wasn't completely under when you treated her. She remembers you using your gift,' she said as she walked over to me and enclosed my hands in hers. 'Go. Now.'

'What about the rest of you?'

'Just get yourself out!'

I sensed the policemen approach before I could see their dark uniforms or hear the deep thud of their boots. Their energies were dark, cold and determined. A young woman trembled between the policemen. Her hand pointed towards me. I recognised her in an instant—she gave birth to twin boys just last Thursday, beautiful bairns they were. But it was a difficult delivery. Perhaps the pain weakened the effect of the anaesthetic spell enough for her to understand how I was helping her.

If only I'd had the chance to show her how we risk our lives each day just to help women like her. She might not have reported me if she had known. Or it may have made no difference at all.

'Where am I supposed to go?' I asked, though my magic urged me to run without a plan.

'Somewhere no one would think to find you. Not even me.' Maisie's voice broke before she could finish and when I focussed on her eyes, they were glazed over with an emotion she rarely showed me. 'Go!'

Despite feeling like my knees would give out, I ran. My thoughts were focussed on escape and trying not to break my ankle in those stupid heels. As I approached a set of doors, they flung open, the handles hitting the wall with an awful cracking sound. Had I done that? My power was surging above the level where I could control it. I knew it had one goal—self-preservation. If I died, so would my magic.

I fell through the final set of doors onto the stone steps. The heat of the sun, now emerging from the darkness of the clouds, fell on my palms. I knew I would be able to feel that moment in all its intensity for however much life remained ahead of me.

My face hit the steps before I had the chance to react. The metallic taste of my own blood was both overpowering and grounding as it flowed into my mouth. The two policemen forced their bodyweight onto my back. They tried to restrain my arms, but I struggled with all my non-magical power. The last thing I wanted to do was give them any more evidence of my gift. Unfortunately, my magic didn't feel the same way.

The jangle of handcuffs closing over my wrists must have been the breaking point. The policeman who held them—a tall, broad man with the most awful moustache—hissed in pain, halting his restraining of my wrists. I turned my head as far as possible to watch him in equal confusion.

'What in God's name...' he said, holding his palm up to his face to inspect.

'What is it, Sir?' the other man said.

'My bloody hand is scorched!' He showed the other man his palm, and they both lessened their grip on me for a moment. It was likely to be the only moment of opportunity I would be given.

I spun around so that I was facing them, my back to the cold steps, and kicked one in the chest and one in the face. They both groaned and I remembered that I was wearing heels—perhaps they weren't so bad after all.

Those same heels were pounding against the pavement before I could process what just happened. I ran in the direction of the Royal Mile, but soon thought better of it. I was running towards the police station, almost straight into their grip. I turned back to the corner I had just come round when the sound of hurried footsteps filled my ears, followed by the deep voice of the moustachioed policeman.

'Iona Thomson, stop!' he said a second before coming into view, the other man a few paces behind.

This was it. I couldn't escape a second time. I swore I could already feel the scratch of the stake, the heat of the flames.

Finally, they had caught a genuine witch.

I disconnected from the tragic scene in front of me, like I was watching it from above. Then came the cracking sound that could only be attributed to human bone. Followed by a scream. The policemen fell to their knees a couple of yards away from me. Their arms and legs twisted in unnatural ways. I couldn't pull my eyes away from them, despite how much I wanted to escape it all.

An all too familiar pulsing flowed through me, and I realised what I had done. Well, not me. What my magic had done. It was out of my control, running on its survival instinct. I tried to move, to help the men, but the pulsing only got stronger. It held me in place as it delivered the final and irreversible blow.

Two snaps. Two thuds.

I tried again to go to them, to use my power for good as I had always strived to do. But it was too late. There was a pool of blood next to the younger man's head. I could've stopped the bleed, but there was no point. The irreversible damage was clear in the angle at which his neck was bent, as well as all four of his limbs. I wasn't sure if it was the years I had spent in the medical field or the remnants of my magic's control that left me numb to the sight in front of me, but it didn't matter either way. They were gone.

The pulsing inside me subsided, but I could still sense it. My magic was exhausted but ready to jump into action if in danger again. I shivered, realising that all the power I'd housed in my body for twenty-three years was no longer under my control.

The clouds grew dark again, and rain soon began its assault on the pavement as I ran. People stopped to give me strange looks, but it didn't faze me. It was a sort of comfort to see something familiar. Buildings blurred at the edges of my vision but I knew the town well enough to know where I was going. Deep down, I knew my destination wasn't anywhere good.

As I ran out of the city, desperately seeking an escape at Granton Harbour, I dreaded when my treasured gift would cause such suffering again.

~

# Acknowledgements

With thanks to Broken Sleep Books for this opportunity.

An additional thank you to Fee Griffin for her ongoing support and encouragement.

LAY OUT YOUR UNREST